D1219576

WITHDRAWN

55 Group-Building Activities for Y[outh]

JUN 1 4 2002   JUL 1 4 2003
SEP 1 8 2002   OCT 0 9 2007
AG 1 8 '11

DATE DUE

FEB 2 7 1998	SEP 2 4 2004		
JUN 2 1 1998			
Aug 4			
MAR 3 0 1999			
APR 2 9 1999			
AUG 0 6 1999			
OCT 1 3 1999			
APR 1 5 2000			
MAY 2 2 2001			
APR			
NOV 2 6 2003			

259.2147
Halverson, Sam

55 group building activities
        for youth

Western District Resource Library
2517 North Main
North Newton, KS 67117

DEMCO

55 Group-Building Activities for Youth

Sam Halverson

Abingdon Press
Nashville

Western District Resource Library
2517 North Main
North Newton, KS 67117

55 GROUP-BUILDING ACTIVITIES FOR YOUTH

Copyright © 1996 by Abingdon Press

ISBN 0-687-00528-0

All rights reserved.

No part of this work may be reproduced or transmitted in any form or by any means, electronic or mechanical, including photocopying and recording, or by any information storage or retrieval system, except as may be expressly permitted by the 1976 Copyright Act or in writing from the publisher. Requests for permission should be addressed to Abingdon Press, P.O. Box 801, 201 Eighth Avenue South, Nashville TN 37202-0801.

This book is printed on recycled, acid-free paper.

Library of Congress Cataloging-in-Publication Data

Halverson, Sam.
    55 group-building activities for youth/Sam Halverson.
        p.   cm.
    Includes index.
    ISBN 0-687-00528-0 (pbk.:alk. paper)
    1. Church group work with youth.   I. Title.
BV4447.H2936   1996
259'.23—dc20   96-20131

Unless otherwise noted, Scripture quotations are from the New Revised Standard Version Bible, Copyright 1989 by the Division of Christian Education of the National Council of the Churches of Christ in the USA. Used by permission.

On page 15, the prayer by Adrian Butash is from *Bless This Food*, Copyright © 1993 by Adrian Butash. Used by permission of Dell Books, a division of Bantam Doubleday Dell Publishing Group, Inc.

96 97 98 99 00 01 02 03 04 05—10 9 8 7 6 5 4 3 2 1

MANUFACTURED IN THE UNITED STATES OF AMERICA

Contents

Introduction

Youth Ministry and Youth Traditions

I remember the time when I was forced to attend Sunday school and church activities, long before it became my job and vocation. When I was in junior high, I spent my first waking hours every Sunday morning thinking of different reasons for not liking church. Just any reason wouldn't do—my reasons had to be good enough to convince my parents (one of whom was a preacher's kid) that I should no longer be forced to go to church.

I struggled for a couple of years with this issue, but never found a solution. Although I don't remember many of the reasons I gave, I do remember an argument I had with a Sunday school teacher one Sunday morn-

ing. I wanted to know why our class had to take part in the children's Christmas pageant. We were too old for such childish things, and I wanted out of the responsibility. "The junior-high class always does this," was the answer. "It's a tradition."

At that point, I began to rebel against traditions. They seemed poor excuses for getting me to do something uninteresting that someone *else* wanted me to do. Why should I be expected to carry out someone else's tradition?

Years later, I realized that it wasn't the traditions that were bad, it was *"someone else's traditions"—traditions that I had no ownership in*—that I hated. Today I can point to dozens of traditions that my junior- and senior-high kids have adopted and claim as their own. Traditions are vital in the lives of youth, and especially in youth ministry. The important thing to remember is that they need to be the youth's traditions. This often means that these customs or traditions are very different from those of any other group in the church. When youth accept ownership of a tradition, community is built within the group, bonding the members to an activity that has meaning, and that defines who they are. If those traditions happen to be Christian, then that helps them define themselves even more.

Traditions give ownership in youth programs and activities.

A youth program that contains the youth's own traditions helps young people see the way the program has been inherently designed for them. They recognize that no other age group or organization in the church sings this particular song or celebrates birthdays in that particular way. They see that the benediction at the end of their meetings is their own, and no other group in the church yells "Praise God" as they sing "Pass It On."

On the other hand, traditions that feel confining, restrictive, or forced will often push teenagers away, rather than bring them together. This is not to say that youth will reject all churchwide traditions or those that encompass a larger segment of the congregation. In fact, churchwide customs may be adopted more quickly than those that have been "molded" specifically to fit the youth group.

Some churchwide customs (such as singing a particular song at the end of the worship service or attending a special Advent service each year) actually embrace youth as well as children and adults, and, rather than being forceful or restrictive, really welcome everyone into the entire church family. A helpful, linking custom welcomes the fellowship of believers like an old favorite chair that has been molded through years of holding our shape and continues to beckon us into its comforting arms.

Traditions create something dependable.

Teenagers want and need to be able to depend on certain things in their lives. So many things in teenagers' world are continually changing—school, friends, fashions, music, their bodies, boyfriends, girlfriends— and sometimes even their families are changing faster than they would like. Although youth like change and things that are new and exciting, they also like to invest time and energy in things that are reliable. If too much is changing too rapidly, teenagers will resist investing much of their time or energy.

When a certain routine is followed at the youth meeting, retreat, or worship service, teenagers are more comfortable (like sitting in that old familiar chair). Friends are more likely to be invited when youth group members know that an event is safe and free from embarrassing surprises. While surprise is good in a youth program, the more traditions a youth can point to that he or she

appreciates, the more trust there is in that program.

Traditions bring back memories.

What immediately comes to mind when you read these traditions:
—setting out cookies for Santa
—carving jack-o'-lanterns
—hunting for eggs at Easter
—a candlelight worship service
—singing "Pass It On"
—receiving a valentine from someone you really like
—the last night at a church camp or retreat

You probably can link a positive memory with each of these customs, yet the practice of those customs began long before the particular events you remember. Traditions link us to certain times that are meaningful. The early Christians began the observance of communion because it linked them to the memory of Christ's last supper; the people of Israel "remembered" (and continue to remember) each time they follow the ritual of the Passover; you might remember a certain special Christmas whenever you participate in singing Christmas carols or sit down for a Thanksgiving meal. In the same way, when youth act out their own rituals or follow their established customs, they will remember events, faces, and relationships that are linked to those same rituals or traditions. Some of those relationships involve family and friends, but when the tradition involves the church, a relationship with God is remembered and enforced.

Traditions link youth to the past and future.

Just as traditions link youth to memories, your youth also will find their customs and traditions connecting them across time— backward and forward. A Christian who participates in the ritual of communion is connected with all the Christians who have communed with Christ before, and all those who will commune in the future. This "communion of the saints" is a part of what unites all Christians—those alive, dead, and yet to be—into the Body of Christ.

I remember my first communion as a youth minister with a new congregation. As I stood before the congregation and began serving people I didn't yet know, I thought of all the people I missed from the church I had left the week before. Then it hit me. It was World Communion Sunday—a Sunday when Christians around the world are encouraged to partake in the holy sacrament. While I was serving the body and blood of Christ at my new church, the congregation was receiving that same body and blood in my old church. I was connected to them through this holy sacrament—this living tradition. Now, whenever I participate in communion, I am reminded of the host of people who share in this privilege—past, present, and future, near and distant, stranger and friend.

While communion is a holy sacrament, the customs and traditions of your youth can bring some of that same connection to the Body of Christ, past, present, and future. When your group realizes that their youth fellowship benediction is perhaps the

same benediction that their youth counselors or parents prayed, and may very well be the same one their children will pray when they become teenagers, a certain vicarious bond exists throughout time and space, linking each member of that fellowship with another.

Getting Started

So how does one start a tradition without "forcing" an activity down teenagers' throats? Well, be on the lookout for times when a "tailor made" custom is in the making. It may be one that is an "offshoot" of a larger congregational tradition. For example, in my church, it is a congregational tradition to worship in our sanctuary every Sunday. Several years ago, our youth decided to sit on the back pew during the worship service. As they continue this practice today, they are participating in the congregational tradition—worshiping on Sundays—but with a unique twist that allows them to remain individuals.

You can help start traditions by bringing ideas to a leadership team of youth and adults, such as a youth council, explaining the significance of youth customs. Or make youth traditions the theme of an upcoming planning meeting or retreat. Ask your retreaters to:

► Name the traditions and customs of your group.

► Talk about why they are important.

► Suggest some new ideas or activities for the group to consider.

Be careful not to introduce too many new traditions at once. The youth may sense too much of a shift and lose faith in the stability of the group.

It will become easier to incorporate new traditions as your years as a youth leader at a church grow. The youth will begin to trust you, and you will better understand the dynamics of your youth and of your ministry.

But new youth workers should not shy away from starting a new practice. Because they have not shared in the established pattern of the group, it is often easier for them to introduce new ideas. Introducing a new way of closing worship time or opening a retreat could be just the touch needed to connect a new youth director with a group. Use the various activities, ideas, and suggestions in the following chapters to build new youth practices and customs, or to add a new twist to your existing ministry.

CHAPTER 1

Youth Meetings

Meetings are a constantly changing event in most youth ministries. Newcomers show up (some of whom have never stepped inside a church before), the more experienced youth eventually graduate and are replaced by inexperienced younger youth, adult leaders and volunteers change, the youth leadership changes, and programs and activities differ each week. In a setting with so much change, youth (and adults) need activities that give structure, meaning, and connection to the unpredictable future.

The following activities can help your youth—new and old, seasoned and rookies, leaders and followers—connect with and take ownership of the program, find meaning in what they do, and discover symbols that speak for the community of faith.

"For where two or three are gathered
in my name, I am there among them."

–Matthew 18:20

The Empty Chair

Use this activity to open a meeting, at the beginning of worship time, or at some type of closing experience. The entire group gathers (standing or sitting) and faces in the same direction (a circle, rows, semicircle, etc.). A single empty chair is conspicuously placed among the group. The leader (youth or adult) explains that the empty chair is there to remind the group of two things:

1. Christ is present with us.
2. Others who need to be here with us are not here today.

Expand on these points, stating that Jesus said that whenever two or more are gathered in his name, there he is also. Other discussion points could include:

1. Elaborate on the second thing by asking who is missing;
2. offer prayers for absent members and friends;
3. ask group members to think of someone who needs to be here and to later tell that person that he or she was missed;
4. write the names of missing persons and call each person during the week.

☼ ☼ ☼ ☼ ☼ Variation ☼ ☼ ☼ ☼ ☼

As this activity becomes an ongoing practice, ask different people to explain what the chair symbolizes (or ask the entire group at once, making it almost a litany). In this way, the tradition becomes a powerful symbol of Christian fellowship and witness.

☼ ☼ ☼ ☼ ☼ ☼ ☼ ☼ ☼ ☼ ☼ ☼ ☼ ☼ ☼ ☼

Circle Up

Welcome everyone into the fellowship of the meeting by forming a connected circle facing inward. Sing a special song, so that everyone knows it is time to start *circling up*. A circle allows everyone to see all the faces that have gathered for the meeting and is a good place to have the opening prayer.

Introducing this idea as a continuous activity is not always easy. Here are a few mixers or games that will bring everyone into a circle:

Amoeba Tag begins with one person who is "it." As this person touches others, they must grab one hand of the "amoeba," which keeps growing and growing as more and more people are touched by the people on the ends of the line. Finally, at the end of the game, everyone is connected in one big line. Then join the two ends, and you have your circle.

In *Prui* (proo´-ee), all the players are blindfolded (or keep their eyes closed) and mix around the room, asking everyone they meet, "prui?" (so that all one hears is the word "prui," stated over and over). One individual, selected as *the Prui*, walks around with eyes open and, when asked, "prui?" does not answer. Instead, he or she quietly takes the person's hand and removes their blindfold (or the person opens their eyes). As the Prui enlarges with more and more people, the room gets quieter and quieter. Eventually, there is one big line of people holding hands in a room, quietly listening to the last person saying "prui? prui?" This is a fun way to make a circle.

✵ ✵ ✵ ✵ ✵ *Variation* ✵ ✵ ✵ ✵ ✵

Ask a few of the leaders in your group to help with forming a circle at the beginning of each meeting. If you begin your meetings with a snack supper or another activity where a line is formed, begin with a circling up activity, then break the circle after your opening prayer, creating the needed line for supper. This is a great way to show that "the last shall be first, and the first shall be last," although some may not like such biblical examples every week.

✵ ✵ ✵ ✵ ✵ ✵ ✵ ✵ ✵ ✵ ✵ ✵ ✵ ✵ ✵

Prayer

Look for ways to invite God into your traditions. Some youth groups always use the same unison prayer or blessing before their meetings. Hang the words to this prayer on the wall, or position them in plain view for newcomers. This invites them into the fellowship of your group. Try using one of the following prayers at your next meeting:

O God, we know you watch over us,
for we have felt your loving presence
throughout the day—protecting, guiding,
and sustaining us. For your constant care
and the blessings of this day, we offer
our gratitude and praise. Amen.

From *Everyday Prayers for Mealtime* (Nashville: Dimensions for Living, 1994), p. 32.

Dearest Lord, teach me to be generous;
Teach me to serve thee as thou deservest;
To give and not to count the cost,
To fight and not to heed the wounds,
To toil and not to seek for rest,
To labour and not to seek reward,
Save that of knowing that I do thy will.

Ignatius of Loyola

Or make your prayer a sung blessing. One example might be the Doxology, or if it is a blessing before a meal, the Wesleyan Blessing, sung to the tune of the Doxology:

The Doxology
Praise God from whom all blessings flow.
Praise him all creatures here below.
Praise him above, ye heavenly host.
Praise Father, Son, and Holy Ghost.
Amen.

The Wesleyan Blessing
Be present at our table, Lord.
Be here and everywhere adored.
Thy mercies bless and grant that we
May feast in fellowship with thee.
Amen.

Here are other blessings that can be spoken or sung:

So often bread is taken for granted,
Yet there is so much of beauty in bread—
Beauty of the sun and the soil,
Beauty of human toil.
Winds and rains have caressed it,
Christ, Himself, blessed it.

From Adrian Butash, *Bless This Food*

Though we sit at the table, may we have the spirit of the one who serves. We ask through Christ, who was among us as one who served. Amen.

From *Everyday Prayers for Mealtime* (Nashville: Dimensions for Living, 1994), p. 63.

The Blessing of God
rest upon all those who have been kind to
    us,
have cared for us, have worked for us,
have served us,
and have shared bread with us at this
    table.
Our merciful God,
reward all of them in your
    own way.
For yours is the glory and
    honor forever. Amen.

Saint Cyril of the Coptic Orthodox Church

The words of a prayer can be sung to many tunes, including "Amazing Grace," the theme from *The Pink Panther* or *M*A*S*H,* the Gillette jingle

(that's an old one!), or "Mary Had a Little Lamb." Have a contest to think of tunes that fit the words of your blessing, and then vote on the one your group wants to adopt as its melody. Or ask group members to write a prayer and put it to music, with each age level composing its own song/prayer. You could use a different prayer each week, rotating among all that were written.

Athletic/Recreation Event

The youth group of which I was a member began every meeting with a game of football (in the fall and winter) or softball (in the spring and summer). We were a small group, and I later learned that the counselors especially liked our games because we burned off loads of energy before the meeting, making us more "teachable" by the time the program began. Beginning meetings in this way helps to build teamwork and cooperation into the program before you even begin. As latecomers arrive, put them immediately into the game (if they want to play). Adults should participate, too, although they need not actually play the game. To get started, organize a recreation committee of youth who will decide what game to play and will promote it, so that people will want to arrive on time.

Don't limit your choices to football and softball. Volleyball and Capture the Flag are good for getting everyone involved. They allow for additions of latecomers without disrupting the game. Consider lesser known games like Ultimate Frisbee (similar to football, but with a Frisbee), Manhunt, or Sardines (each with a twist on the classic hide and seek). Some good resources for a variety of group games are *Play It!* and *Play It Again!* by Wayne Rice and Mike Yaconelli.

Be careful that games don't become exclusionary. Kids who are more coordinated and better at playing certain sports may end up intimidating others without even realizing it. Be conscious of fairness, and don't let captains "pick" teams, because someone always gets picked last. Encourage members who don't wish to play to join the game by watching and cheering. Consider having one grade play against another grade, so that the cheerleaders can root for their own grade.

Worship

While worship is a practice that the entire Body of Christ shares, it should also be one that your youth adopts as its own. This can be done by offering a short time of worship at

each youth meeting that is different from the Sunday morning services of the entire congregation. Teenagers need to know that they can worship God in their own way and that God is a God for every age. Invite participation by asking group members to lead the music, offer prayers, read scripture, or provide the message. Make each service creative and unique.

As the youth become familiar with conducting the service, organize a worship committee composed of teenagers and adults who meet regularly to plan and carry out the worship ideas gathered from your meetings. Don't be surprised if these services entice a few adults to attend your youth worship activities.

Songs

Songs make great traditions. Although they don't always have to be sung during worship, they add a great deal to the worship experience. Songs can spark memories, signal an upcoming activity, and alter the mood of a group by getting it moving or quiet. The next time you are riding with a group of kids in a car or van, and a well-known song begins to play, ask everyone to talk about the memory that song brings to mind. Our minds automatically recall pictures, smells, images, and experiences when we hear a familiar tune. If the music sung or played at your youth meetings is linked to past retreats, mission trips, certain worship services, particular topics, or other special moments, it is more likely to carry an important meaning. A frequently used song or tune will help the group gel more quickly, adding meaning and memory to the experience.

Ask several teenagers to accompany the songs on various instruments: guitar, drums, piano, harmonica, or even spoons. Their participation will strengthen their connection to the group and link more memories to particular songs and meetings.

Use certain songs for different parts of the worship experience. For example, a well-known song during communion or altar time allows everyone to sing along without needing a song book or sheet; a well-known tune played or sung softly before the message tells your group to prepare for the upcoming message; opening worship with the same praise song alerts everyone that worship has begun; and closing worship with a sung benediction can send worshipers forth with confidence that they are the children of God.

If your group likes to sing, making a song a customary practice should be no problem (as long as the song is one your group likes to sing). On the other hand, if you have trouble getting your group to sing, try using a tape or a soloist. Capitalize on a special experience (like a retreat) where the group may be more inclined to learn a new song. Later, during your regular meetings, when the song is reintroduced, your members will be more willing to sing, since it will remind them of that special retreat experience.

Prayer and Altar Time

Prayer is a great vehicle for tradition. Many youth groups have a prayer time during a closing circle, joining hands while offering a prayer at the altar. Wherever and however you choose to have your closing prayer, provide a place and a method that allows youth to feel comfortable while worshiping and praying.

Creating a habit of meeting God at the altar helps youth become more comfortable in the sanctuary and at the altar. Offering prayer in a closing circle in a regular meeting room or outdoors teaches youth that any place can be holy, since God exists everywhere.

Sharing joys and concerns during prayer time introduces youth to caring for the community. Teenagers like to know that others are aware of their struggles, concerns, and celebrations. Offer a time during the worship service for people to verbalize expressions of concern and thanks to God. Don't be afraid of the silence that may exist during this time. Just remind everyone to think of their joys and concerns and share them in prayer, if they'd like. One way to help young people feel more comfortable in verbalizing their prayers is to "plant" two to five young people to offer their prayers for the first month or so.

Sharing concerns also can be done at the beginning of the youth meeting. This helps everyone learn what's been going on with group members during the past week. As the meeting progresses, people already will be aware of many of the concerns on group members' minds.

The following is another way to help teenagers feel comfortable while praying aloud for each other:

1. Hand out slips of paper at the beginning of the meeting.
2. Ask each person to write a prayer concern or celebration on the paper, but ask that it not be signed.
3. Collect the papers.
4. Before your closing worship time or prayer, distribute the papers at random.
5. Start the prayer by asking God to listen as people share the joys and concerns of the group.

6. Ask each person to read aloud the concerns or joys that are written on their paper.

7. Close after everyone has had an opportunity to read and speak.

Closings

Crossing Arms in a Closing Circle

At the closing of your meeting, it is important to put an "ending" on your time together. Gathering in a circle allows everyone to see the entire group. Ask each individual to cross the right arm over the left arm, and then join hands. This creates a cross in front, reminding everyone that Christ goes with them. It also links them together, reminding them that each one is a part of the Body of Christ. When you have finished with a benediction, prayer, or closing announcement, ask the entire group to continue holding hands and "unwrap" themselves, causing the entire circle to face in the opposite direction. This is a reminder that they are to take Christ with them as they go their separate ways.

Leaving an Opening in the Closing Circle

Try using the closing circle with everyone holding hands (or even crossing arms), except for one gap left in the circle. Tell the youth that this opening is a reminder that:

1. This is not a closed group, and others are always welcome to join.
2. We are connected to Christians everywhere (both in the past and in the future).
3. Christ is present in the circle.

Benediction

Traditionally, Christians close their meetings with a benediction. Often, the leader offers the benediction, asking for God's blessing on each person as they continue in their daily lives or in Christ's ministry. Using the same benediction at the end of every meeting builds a powerful bond, connecting each generation of youth and each individual with memories of past retreats, meetings,

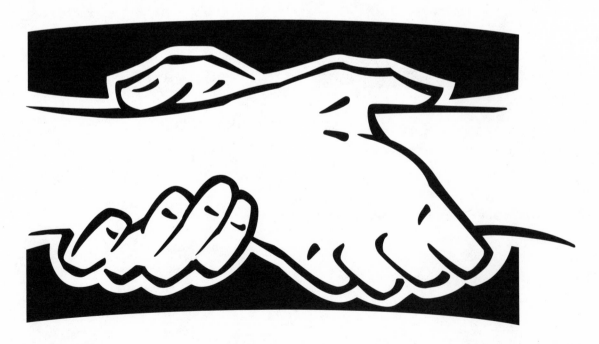

and worship times.

Consider having the youth create such a benediction themselves. Another possibility is to have the senior class write one each year. Many groups use a scripture passage from the Bible. One common benediction (and common is good here, because it reminds youth that it is "their" benediction whenever they hear it or read it) can be found in Numbers 6:24-26. At the end of a chapter filled with rules for the nazirites is this priestly blessing:

> The LORD bless you and keep you;
> the LORD make his face to shine upon
>   you, and be gracious unto you;
> the LORD lift up his countenance upon
>   you, and give you peace.

Explain that God gave this blessing thousands of years ago to the high priest, Aaron, commanding him and all his priests to use it. God said that if the blessing was pronounced upon the people of God, then God would bless them. This (or any other blessing from the scriptures) connects your youth not only with other Christians from the past, but also with scripture. If the scripture you choose is taken from the Old Testament, the youth are connected with the ancient Israelites.

Remember that a benediction is not always a prayer, so the youth don't always need to bow their heads and close their eyes. If it is a blessing spoken to the people (such as the one from Numbers) then encourage the youth to look at one another and give the blessing to one another. Recently our youth adopted the above blessing and began looking into the eyes of others in the circle as they recite in unison, emphasizing the words *you* throughout the benediction. Each time they say *you,* they nod to a particular person, catching his or her eye and stating that part of the blessing. This new custom has emerged over time and is a new twist on an ancient tradition.

CHAPTER 2

Retreats

In 1994, 1,000 teenagers who attended a Christian youth convention in Washington D.C. were asked to name the deciding factor in their decision to follow Christ. A majority responded that they made a commitment to Christ after a particular experience at a youth retreat.

This shouldn't be surprising. Throughout the Bible, people found great wisdom and made huge leaps in their faith on retreats. Moses received the Ten Commandments during his retreat on Mount Sinai, and Elijah found God in a still, small voice after retreating to the wilderness. Although Jonah's retreat into the whale's belly was forced upon him, he repented and recognized his responsibility and duty to God. Peter, John, and James witnessed Jesus' transfiguration when they retreated with him to a mountaintop. Jesus took numerous personal retreats to rest and pray before taking his next step in ministry.

Retreats take us away from our daily schedule and routine. They interrupt our lives, allowing the Holy Spirit to enter and change our lives permanently. Youth who experience a Christian retreat are given an opportunity to refocus their lives and priorities. Adults who plan and lead youth retreats are given an opportunity to be used by God as communicators of the gospel and agents of the Holy Spirit.

Unfortunately, retreats also can be hectic and dysfunctional. Sometimes youth are more focused on "running rampant" than on developing their faith. However, incorporating inspirational activities and practices into your retreat can provide moments of reflection and redirection for participants, and are generally easy to introduce. If an activity works well, a few teenagers will want to do it during every retreat.

You may even want to establish a retreat planning committee composed of young people. Each time you find success with one of the ideas that follow, pass it on to the committee for the next retreat. This practice soon will evolve into your youth taking ownership of their retreats and the meaningful, spiritual experiences that they provide.

I had heard of you by the
hearing of the ear,
but now my eye sees you.

–Job 42:5

Secret Pals

Introducing secret pals into a retreat experience encourages youth to give and also receive affirmation. Here's how the process works:

1. Write the names of each retreat participant on a separate envelope.
2. Shuffle the envelopes so they are in random order.
3. Copy the names from the envelopes (in the same order as the shuffled envelopes) onto small slips of paper—one name per slip.
4. Place one slip inside each envelope. The name inside the first envelope should be the name that appears on the front of the second envelope; the name inside the second envelope should be the name that appears on the front of the third envelope, and so on. This process continues until the name inside the last envelope is the same one that appears on the outside of the first envelope.
5. Make a master list of who is writing to whom and give it to one adult on the retreat. If someone does not write, this person will know who is responsible.
6. Explain that everyone will receive an envelope with a name inside, and that name is to be kept secret.
7. Throughout the retreat, each person will write affirming letters to the secret pal at least twice a day. The writers can write about characteristics they admire in their pal or what they enjoy about the retreat. The letters should not be signed.

Supply pens, paper, and a mailbox. Instead of a centrally located mailbox, hang individual mailboxes (large envelopes with participants' names on them) on a wall in the main meeting room. This allows the pals to pick up their mail whenever they like, rather than waiting for "mail call."

Allow time during the retreat closing for the secret pals to reveal themselves. This can be done individually by telling everyone to take the left hand of the person to whom they were writing. This results in everyone standing in a circle, and you can move immediately into a closing prayer or benediction.

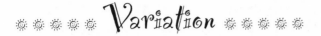

If your group is small, ask the participants to share brief comments about their secret pals before mentioning the names. In this way, each person is affirmed in front of the entire group.

Secret pals takes a little effort, but is extremely rewarding, and is easily led by an adult or youth volunteer. You may find that your youth are asking for secret pals at every retreat, saying, "It's a tradition."

Agape

The Greeks had many different words for love—each signifying a different type of love. The word *agape* means Christian love, something which should be shown and given every time the Body of Christ meets, whether as a group of youth on a retreat or as a whole family of faith gathered for worship.

Agape is also a word used to describe unexpected gifts given during retreats to each participant by other members of the faith community. These gifts can range from prayer chains and letters to snack food and small favors. The more creative the gift, the more surprising the *agape*.

But the gifts are more than mere "presents." They are symbols of God's love. For example, a roll of Lifesavers might be left on each person's pillow, with an attached note: "Jesus saves your life . . . eternally." A bowl of goldfish crackers might be set on a meeting table with a label: "I will make you fishers of men," and signed "Jesus."

Using the above scripture, blunted fish hooks hanging on a fishing net could be brought into the retreat meeting room. Or someone dressed as a fisherman could give a little comic speech before handing out the hooks to each youth. The scripture verse would be attached to each fish hook.

One powerful agape for a youth group is to discover, halfway through the retreat, that their parents have been keeping a continuous prayer vigil for the retreaters throughout the entire weekend.

Agape gifts are new and creative ways to introduce the gospel to young people, and it's easy to get an agape program started for your next retreat.

When planning your retreat, ask two to five young people to work with one adult on an agape team. They are to:

▶ Think up creative ways of communicating Christian love to the retreat participants.
▶ Remain anonymous from the retreat participants until the retreat. Secrecy adds to the fun of the team and helps the tradition continue year after year.
▶ Receive the schedule for the entire retreat, since there will be certain times that agape will have a stronger impact on the retreaters. For example, agape is a great way to break up long periods of sitting. A good way to drive a message home after an important talk or dinner is to interrupt with something funny, yet meaningful. The agape team could set gifts at the table for each meal and on each per-

son's pillow each evening. If any long talks or sessions are planned, suggest that the agape team noisily interrupt the meeting at a predetermined time, to hand out some sort of agape pertaining to a key message of the retreat.

One youth group takes great joy in planning its interruptions. The agape team dresses up in costume and acts out a skit while handing out (or throwing out) the agape.

Another dimension to the agape tradition is to ask various organizations in your church to prepare agape for the retreat. The youth might receive pocket crosses from an adult Sunday school class, cookies in the shape of butterflies from the women's group, a pair of dice (Christ is preparing "paradise" for you) from the choir, and a copy of the "Footprints" poem typed on a card from the pastor. Families, church staff, and Sunday school classes can get involved as well by making crosses, writing scriptures, and preparing food. The youth not only will be reminded of God's love, but that love also will be linked to the church family.

Here are a few more agape ideas:

Prayer Rocks

A small rock tied in a piece of cloth is attached to this note:

I'm your little prayer rock, and this is what
I'll do;
Just put me on your pillow until the day is
through.
Then turn back the covers and climb into
your bed,
And WHACK, your little prayer rock will hit
you on the head.

Then you will remember just as the day is
through,
To kneel and say your prayers as you had wanted
to.
Then, after you are finished, just drop me on the
floor.
I'll stay there through the nighttime, to give you
help once more.
When you get up next morning, CLUNK, I'll
stub your toe
So you'll remember your morning prayers before
you go.
Put me back upon your pillow when your bed is
made,
And your little prayer rock will continue in your
aid.
Because the Lord, Christ Jesus cares and loves
you so,
He wants you to remember to talk to God, you
know!

Pocket Crosses

These are small crosses that can be carried inside a pocket or purse. They can be purchased in most Christian bookstores or ordered through church supply catalogues. Or you could experiment with simple nails and glue. Try to find a box of flat or square nails. Be sure to blunt the nails, since sharp points will tear a hole in most any pocket. Use four nails per cross. Two nails, facing in opposite directions, are glued together to form the crosspiece of the cross. Two other nails, also facing in opposite directions, but glued so that they lie a little longer, make up the vertical stand of the cross. When that glue has dried, the vertical and horizontal pieces can be glued together.

Letters from Home

It's often a surprise to get mail while on a retreat, but when the letters are affirming and positive, it's a very pleasant surprise. The agape team can ask each parent to secretly write a letter to their teen before the retreat. The letters should be affirming and communicate their love for their child. At a key point during the retreat, deliver the letters, and allow time for them to be read. Be sure that there are letters for every participant, since it hurts to be left out.

Calendars

These can be fancy or plain. Small pocket calendars can often be purchased in bulk from bookstores or print shops at very low cost. Wall calendars can be made using a computer program, drawn by hand, or photocopied. Write all the youth activities on each calendar—including the weekly youth meetings, special Sundays, and upcoming retreats and special events. If possible, also note all retreaters' birthdays (or those of everyone in your youth group). Wrap the calendars with a note: "And lo, I am with you always. Even to the close of the age."—Jesus

Pretzels

This common snack has a tradition and story all its own. Centuries ago, a monastery used to bake these specially shaped breaded treats to remind people of a life of prayer and worship. The shape of the pretzel is similar to the shape of one's arms when they are folded and crossed humbly in prayer. Tell the story of the pretzel as you hand out bags, bowls, or even fresh-baked pretzels. Don't forget the mustard!

Letters from Other Youth Groups

Ask the youth minister of another youth group to announce that your group is going on a retreat soon. If possible, also send the youth minister the names of the retreat participants. First, ask the youth at the other church to:

1. Pray for your group, asking God to direct the retreat, and especially the minds and hearts of the retreaters.
2. Write a letter or make a poster, telling your group that they are being prayed for during the retreat. If names are sent, the other group could write each retreat participant a letter, affirming them in their faith growth.

During the retreat, distribute the letters or unveil the poster, explaining what the youth from the other group are doing while your group is on this retreat. This is a great way to show Christian love from other brothers and sisters in Christ. Offer to reciprocate the prayers, letters, or poster for the other youth group when they go on a retreat.

Mail

Don't discount the obvious in planning your agape program. There are people in the church and community who can be powerful resources for your next retreat. The New Testament is full of letters written to Christians, affirming and guiding them in their walk with Christ. Such letters have continued to bring guidance, motivation, direction, and inspiration to countless souls since they were written.

The next time you plan a retreat, give the agape team a list of the youth who will attend. Have the team contact parents of the retreaters, asking for the names and addresses of the significant people in their teenagers' life. To those peo-

ple, send a letter similar to the one below.

Distribute the letters at a key point in the retreat—after a meal, following a meaningful talk, or at the Sunday morning worship service. Be ready for tears and lots of smiles.

Junior Counselors

Some retreats may be designed specifically for younger youth. For example, a confirmation retreat is ideal for a seventh-grade confirmation class, or the sixth-, seventh-, and eighth-graders may have their own retreat experience separately from the high schoolers. Often the younger youth have no prior retreat experience and look toward others who know what to expect. In addition, younger youth typically look up to older youth, and when they are not present, an important faction of leadership is missing.

Before your next retreat for the younger youth, train a handful of older youth to be junior counselors. Keep the number of counselors small, or the retreat will begin to resemble a mixed, all-age retreat, rather than one designed specifically for younger youth.

Junior counselors will need to understand their responsibilities and their limits regarding instruction and discipline. As counselors, older teens develop

---

Dear friend or family of _____,
_____ is registered for our upcoming retreat on October 27-29 at Camp Blessing. It should be an enjoyable and meaningful weekend. During part of that time, he/she will be receiving letters from friends, relatives, teachers, coaches, and ministers. That's where you come in. Your name has been mentioned as someone who might wish to participate in our retreat by writing a letter to _____, affirming him/her and letting him/her know of your support. The letter need not be long, but heartfelt (and a secret).

I hope you'll help. The more letters _____ gets, the more surprised he/she will be.

I will need your letter by _____. Please write _____'s name on the outside of the envelope. If you have any questions, please call me at _____.

Thank you for your help.

In Christ,
Youth Minister

---

strong ties with younger youth, and the younger youth witness leadership skills and a quality of faith that they will want to achieve themselves. Soon the older youth may ask whether you plan to have junior counselors at every retreat, and the younger youth will begin to look forward to carrying on the tradition when they are older.

Campfires

There's nothing like a fire and a group of friends bound together by Christ to draw everyone into an atmosphere of fellowship. An evening campfire on a retreat is just what's needed to take the chill off the night and put some warmth into everyone's weekend.

Begin planning for the campfire early in the retreat (or assign the project to a team).

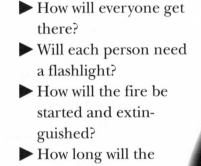

▶ Where will the campfire be?
▶ How will everyone get there?
▶ Will each person need a flashlight?
▶ How will the fire be started and extinguished?
▶ How long will the campfire last?
▶ What type of mood should be established?
▶ Will there be music? Storytelling? Food?

Wood and kindling will need to be collected early and kept dry. Ask someone to set the wood earlier in the day, so that all you need to do is ignite it.

Many groups provide snack food (popcorn or chips) at a campfire. Others are not satisfied unless there are marshmallows to roast. Since the food will distract everyone's attention, distribute it after the talk, singing, or storytelling.

Sometimes campfires are used as places to "chronicle" the youth group. Specific adults and youth are asked to talk about special moments in the history of the youth group. They are asked to focus on the ways the Holy Spirit has been involved in the lives of youth group members, or to recount youth outings and experiences that exhibited God's presence. This type of storytelling resembles the campfires of ancient days, when the biblical stories of creation and the patriarchs were told and retold. This oral tradition emphasizes the community and strengthens the bond of fellowship among group members.

T-shirts

Powerful talks, water fights, long nights, early mornings, quiet hikes, noisy hikes, fun songs, campfires, girls, guys, tears, new commitments—these are some of the things that add to retreat memories. Whenever we're reminded of past retreats, we remember a few of the occurrences that took place. A T-shirt can serve as a constant reminder of that special time. Imagination and creativity for a one- or two-color design is really all you need for a T-shirt that your kids will wear again and again.

Many church youth groups include the cost of printing their own personally designed T-shirt into the registration cost of a retreat. The design need not be extravagant, and shirts bought in bulk can be quite cost-effective. You could even purchase shirts in bulk with other youth groups in your area. This also would help develop professional relationships with other group leaders.

Or consider saving printing costs by asking a parent to decorate shirts with T-shirt paints or permanent markers. T-shirt decoration also could be an activity on a retreat, calling on the creaivity of your group. If the group members wear the shirts to school, they're more likely to talk about the trip, and remember again the fun and faith growth they experienced during the retreat. As the years pass, and your youth collect several shirts from a variety of retreats, they will be able to draw upon the memories of those significant times.

Affirmation Circles

Affirmation circles can easily become an expected practice at all your retreats, because youth enjoy being affirmed and watching others be affirmed.

An affirmation circle involves:

- ▶ a quiet space large enough for everyone to sit in one circle,
- ▶ a candle, and
- ▶ at least one to three hours—depending upon the size of your group and the members' willingness to speak up.

After everyone is seated, dim or extinguish the lights. In the middle of the circle, the leader lights the candle in silence, explaining that the only person who can talk is the person holding the candle. Everyone is welcome to come to the middle of the circle and hold the candle while sharing a particular topic, such as what he or she has gained from the retreat so far.

☀ ☀ ☀ ☀ *Variation* ☀ ☀ ☀ ☀

1. *Pass the candle around the circle, asking all the participants to comment on the retreat or on a specific topic (i.e., how they have experienced God lately, what they learned during the retreat, how they want their lives to change, etc.). If there is time after the candle has traveled around the entire circle, allow people to take the candle again and continue to share.*

2. *If your group numbers less than twenty, try this:*

1. **Have one person sit in the middle of the circle.**
2. **Pass the candle around, asking each person to say something affirming and uplifting about that person.**
3. **Ask the person being affirmed about any concerns the group could pray about.**
4. **Gather around the youth being affirmed, and ask one person to say a prayer for him or her.**

Do this for everyone in the circle. The process may take a long time, but it is very affirming and builds trust and security within the group.

The right location is key for an affirmation circle. The setting should foster respect, privacy, silence, and worship. Outdoor locations can present problems if the weather is uncomfortable or bugs are a nuisance. While a secluded beach might seem ideal, the waves could become too noisy, or the wind too strong for the candle.

Prayer

Too often as we pack the vans and buses and attempt to remember last minute details before leaving for a retreat, we forget to begin the journey with a prayer. We're so wrapped up in saying good-bye to parents and hoping we've done everything, we neglect to do the first thing needed.

Embarking on a spiritual retreat means that you are seeking ways the Holy Spirit can touch your life and the lives of others on the trip. Make that known—to God as well as to retreaters. No matter how rushed you are to get out of the parking lot, stop, gather together—with the participants, parents, and church staff—and ask God's blessings and direction on this retreat experience. Pray for safety, God's presence to be felt, and that God will use your time together to God's glory. Allow a time for the youth to add their concerns.

Remember also to gather again after the retreat to thank God for the time together and for the strength and insight to remain faithful as you come down from "the mountaintop."

Rules

Every retreat needs rules, because they provide structure and direction. Since adolescence is typically an age when rules and authority are rebelled against or resisted, it is critical to help retreat participants understand the importance of and the reasoning behind establishing and following rules. When youth know their boundaries and the reasons for them, they are more likely to remain within them.

For example, when my youth group takes a choir tour, sometimes all the members sleep in the gym at the host church. The boys sleep on one side of the room and the girls sleep on the other side. Each year a teen will say, "You don't trust us, do you?" So we explain that the issue is not one of trust but of accountability to their parents. If word reached those parents that their sons and daughters had slept together, our choir would not be allowed to take another trip. The rules are there to protect the youth and to ensure that we can take more trips.

The easiest way to instill respect in your youth for retreat rules is by including them in the rule-making process. Start by establishing a committee composed of both youth and parents who will develop a set of general rules for every trip. These should include your church's policy regarding tobacco, drugs, alcohol, and so on.

The presentation of the rules is another area where teenagers can have ongoing participation. A presentation could take the form of a humorous skit, a song, video, slides, or creatively getting everyone to say the rules out loud.

Try writing a litany that can be read aloud by the entire group before the event. This offers a serious commitment to the rules. You also could add humor by leading the group in reading the rules aloud without showing your teeth (or holding your tongue, speaking in pig latin, or keeping your tongue on the roof of your mouth).

CHAPTER 3

Outings and Road Trips

There's something about traveling as a group that draws people together. The journey provides many opportunities to develop lasting memories. Sometimes the long bus ride is the most bonding part of a trip. One summer my youth group traveled to a "destination unknown." The youth were never told where we were going. They were instructed to dress in clothing they didn't mind getting wet, bring a lunch, and plan on being away all day. We piled into the van and began a two and a half hour ride to a distant rock slide in the mountains. We actually spent more time in the van than we did at the rock slide, but the kids loved the trip because they established some great friendships and had loads of fun. Several weeks after the trip, they continued to tell one another stories and "inside" jokes.

Outings to *known* destinations can provide ample opportunities for your youth to establish their group's customs and patterns. Use several of the following ideas on your next road trip.

Let no one despise your youth,
but set the believer an example
in speech and conduct,
in love, in faith, in purity.

–1 Timothy 4:12

Cheering

On long driving trips you will need to stop for gas, food, and restroom breaks. It can be fun to give your youth (especially the stragglers) a reason to get back on the bus, van, or car as soon as possible. Start the practice of cheering as people climb back into the vehicle. While you're waiting for group members to leave the food counter and get back on board, tell those who arrive first to yell and cheer when the others reach the vehicle. If cheering becomes a habit, you might be the one being cheered on your next road trip.

Pictures

Photo Album

Recruit a teenager or youth volunteer to take pictures at all your youth activities (especially retreats and important events). Ask another volunteer to maintain your group's photo album once a month. If you have an active group, you will soon fill several albums. Label the albums with the dates or events covered inside and put them in an accessible location. Pretty soon, you'll find your youth crowded around an album, reliving memories of past trips and activities.

Also try these ideas:

▶ Add captions to the pictures by taping a small white circle next to the person in the photo, making it look as if he or she is speaking the words in the circle.

▶ Print a caption at the bottom of each picture. The captions need not have anything to do with the actual event. The more humorous they are, the better.

Wall of Memories

Designate one wall of your church on which you hang enlargements of pictures of particular events. Continue to add new pictures to your wall each year. It's fun to look at how the kids have grown and changed over time. I have a wall of photos in my office. Whenever kids see the wall, they begin to reminisce about past trips and events. It's a great conversation starter.

☼ ☼ ☼ ☼ ☼ Variation ☼ ☼ ☼ ☼ ☼

Photo walls can be used also in individual classrooms. The seventh-grade classroom, for example, could showcase pictures of past and present seventh-graders. The kids currently in the seventh grade will see pictures of older youth when they were their age.

☼ ☼ ☼ ☼ ☼ ☼ ☼ ☼ ☼ ☼ ☼ ☼ ☼ ☼ ☼ ☼

Slide Show

Designate one night each month or quarter to show slides or a video of past youth activities. Kids often enjoy seeing themselves or their friends on screen. As this becomes a regular event, your youth will make a point of attending so they can see their events being featured. A few youth groups visit local high school football games every Friday night to videotape or photograph the teenagers in the stands. The teens are invited to a screening of themselves on the following Sunday night. This is an activity with strong outreach possibilities.

Photo/Video Scavenger Hunts

Scavenger hunts can offer excitement, a memorable road trip, and photography, all in the same package.

Use reservations to determine how many people will be participating. Solicit several adults to drive the youth around the neighborhood. You will need a vehicle, camera, and film for each vehicle.

You will need to decide whether to use videos or photographs. The use of video gives this activity an interesting twist, but video cameras may be difficult to acquire, since people usually are reluctant to loan such expensive equipment. One major benefit of photographs is that you do not need a VCR and TV to view them. Just pull out the pictures and travel down memory lane. Next, make a list of public places and interesting situations where youth group members must place themselves for the video or photographs. Assign points to the different situations. Give more points for "risky" or difficult shots. Here are some examples:

▶ Everyone in the group standing behind the counter at a nearby fast-food place. (10 pts.) An extra 5 points if everyone is wearing a hat from the restaurant. One additional point for every "stranger" posing in the picture.

▶ Everyone in the group making a human pyramid on aisle 7 in the local supermarket. (15 pts.) (If using video, for an extra 5 points, tell them to sing a particular song while holding the pyramid.)

▶ Again for video: A stranger whistling the theme from "The Andy Griffith Show," while standing in the checkout line at a local grocery store. (15 pts.)

▶ A "fire drill" at a local fast-food establishment drive-thru window. (10 pts.) (See chapter 7 for more information).

▶ The entire group hanging upside down from the football goalposts at the high school football field. (10 pts.)

▶ The whole group in a jail cell at the local police station. (15 pts.)

The wackier the ideas, the more memories your youth will take away from this event, and the more likely the event will be repeated and enjoyed year after year. A big bonus of scavenger hunts is that the kids form strong bonds with one another, and also with the adults who chaperon their group. In addition, they will link locations in the community with their church youth group activities, and showcase the activities of the group to the rest of the community. Remind the hunting parties of this last point before leaving the church, to ensure that everyone represents the church in a courteous manner.

CHAPTER 4

The Seasons

When we think of traditions during the Christmas season, visions of giving gifts, singing carols, visiting with friends and relatives, decorating houses and trees, setting up nativity scenes, and eating lots of yummy food and desserts come to mind. We think of turkey and all its trimmings at Thanksgiving, and for Easter, egg hunts and special worship services. The beginning of the year is a time when many of us look toward new goals and resolutions.

Teenagers rarely tire of annual seasonal routines and customs because of their short duration. In this chapter are numerous activities that your group may be willing to adopt or add to its present long-standing holiday practices.

For everything there is a season,
and a time for every matter
under heaven.

–Ecclesiastes 3:1

Gift Exchanges

For many of us, Christmas is synonymous with gifts and gift giving. Using gift giving as a part of your youth ministry is not only festive, but also illustrates the gospel, if used as an opportunity to teach the scripture. Here are a few of the many analogies you can point to:

▶ the wise men bearing gifts of gold, frankincense, and myrrh for the baby Jesus;

▶ God's tremendous love for the world we have been given as a gift;

▶ the gift of God's only son, Jesus; or

▶ the many gifts of the Holy Spirit, the greatest of which is love.

Create-A-Gift

Rather than following the same old routine of exchanging names and asking everyone to spend no more than $5 for a gift, ask your youth to create their gifts, using their own talents. A list of creative gifts they can make or provide might include:

▶ **performing a full day of chores around the recipient's house**
▶ **a tape with music performed by the giver**
▶ **a framed picture or piece of artwork created by the giver**
▶ **a home-cooked meal, candy, or cookies**
▶ **music lessons given by someone who is musically inclined**
▶ **a drive in the country**

White Elephants

Another variation of inexpensive gift giving is to ask everyone to bring an unwanted, wrapped gift from home to give as a gag gift or white elephant. Number slips of paper from one to the total number of gifts. Place the slips in a hat or bowl, and let each person select a number.

The person with the *number 1* chooses the first gift. After the gift has been opened and shown to the group, the person with the *number 2* can either "steal" the gift from *number 1,* or choose an unopened gift.

The person with the *number 3* has the option of stealing gifts from the people with numbers 1 or 2, or choosing an unopened gift. This process continues until all the gifts have been selected. If a person's opened gift is "stolen" by someone with a higher number, that person selects another unopened gift and unwraps it. After all the gifts have been opened, the first player is given the opportunity to "steal" any gift he or she chooses.

White elephant exchanges are more fun if the gifts are gag gifts and basically worthless to the group. Some of these gifts become traditions in themselves, showing up year after year.

Gift Letters

One unique way of emphasizing gift giving is by affirming the gifts that others have already received from God through their talents, blessings, and gifts of the Spirit. After exchanging names, give your youth a week or two to compose a letter to their gift recipient, affirming that person's talents and gifts.

Secret Santa

Have a "secret Santa" gift exchange. Draw names from a hat or bowl. For a month, each youth member gives gifts or treats to the person whose name he or she drew. The gifts should cost *no* money and be unsigned. Do not reveal the Santas. This illustrates that the joy is truly in giving.

Caroling

Christmas caroling offers an opportunity to spread Christmas cheer and goodwill. Caroling not only provides the chance to sing the gospel, but also to act it out by bringing joy and kindness into the lives of others.

Christmas Serenade

My mother tells of a caroling tradition from her youth. Each year after the candlelight service, the adults in her church held Christmas Eve parties that lasted most of the night. Then early Christmas morning, the youth would sing at the doors of the homes where those parties were just ending. Through their singing, the youth welcomed the morning and the coming of the Savior on Christmas Day. If the adult Sunday school classes in your church have Christmas gatherings, the youth group could start a practice of caroling the partygoers. This is a way to connect them to other groups in the church community.

Carol Outreach

Many youth groups carol each year in local nursing homes or hospitals, mixing outreach and mission with the Christmas season. Other groups visit the homes of church members or simply sing door to door in familiar neighborhoods. One year our youth sang at the homes of our church's Sunday school teachers, letting them know they were appreciated. Another year, we caroled at the homes of our shut-in members.

Family Night

Sponsor a "family night of caroling," and invite church members of all ages to come join the fun. Set the registration deadline for the week prior to your caroling date, in order to arrange adequate transportation. This activity is a wonderful way to showcase your youth. You may even find several older church members willing to volunteer for future youth projects.

Outreach

Since the true meaning of the Christmas season is about bringing good cheer and the gospel to the world, it's only natural to begin thinking about how to reach out to others who are in need. If your youth group doesn't already have an annual Christmas outreach project, use one of the ideas that follow.

The first step is to identify where there is a need:

▶ Are there low-income families near your church?
▶ Is there a homeless or domestic violence shelter nearby?
▶ Are there families in your community that cannot afford Christmas presents?
▶ Do low-income families need help with child care?

Consider collecting toys each Sunday for children of low-income families, or children living in homeless or domestic violence shelters. Find out the ages and gender of the children, and perhaps what they would like for Christmas. List this information in the church bulletin or newsletter (omit the names of the children). Ask church members to purchase new items and bring them to church the following Sundays. Deliver the presents before Christmas (or perhaps at a Christmas party held for the children). Suggest that people spend at least one tenth of what they spend on their own children's Christmas gifts, as a "tithe" for gift giving.

Adopt-A-Child

Ask a social service agency in your community for help in finding the names of children who will need help in purchasing gifts for their parents, brothers, and sisters. Make a list of names and ages of each child, along with their family members. Raise the money for the shopping trip through an outreach or service project. On the day of the shopping trip, pair each child with at least two youth. After all the purchases have been made, help the children wrap their gifts.

Banquet

Food is a perfect complement to the Christmas season, so why not organize a banquet? Many youth groups plan their banquets around traditional Christmas activities. For example, they might go Christmas caroling before the banquet, then exchange gifts after the meal. The banquet can be held in the church, in homes (possibly as a progressive meal), or at a restaurant.

A progressive meal involves different households hosting one course of the meal. The youth and adult leaders first travel to *house A* for the blessing and appetizers. Then they travel to *house B* for salad and soup. Next they go to *house C* for the main course. Finally they move on to *house D* for dessert.

Developing a theme provides a special flair to the event. Try one of these theme ideas: *dress as characters from the Christmas story; select a particular country or culture and highlight its food, decorations, and dress; or focus all the decorations, dress, and activities on Christmas carols.*

A Journey to Bethlehem

Imagine walking the streets and seeing the bazaars of Bethlehem on the night that Mary and Joseph were searching for a place to stay. What sights would you see? What sounds would you hear? What would you smell and feel? Imagine hearing the gruff voice of a Roman soldier commanding you to "move on," or asking if you've been counted in the census yet. Imagine the odor of cow manure mixing with the smell of burning incense, and the sounds of merchants competing for your attention on the crowded streets.

Now imagine the rooms and hallways of your church transformed into the alleys and streets of Bethlehem. Up ahead is an usher dressed as a potter, sitting in his "shop" and molding a set of clay cups. Across the alley are a Sunday school teacher and his family, serving a crowded table of soldiers and travelers in what is usually a classroom but is now a crowded inn. The "beggar" sitting at the side of the street is the senior pastor.

This is an activity in which the entire church can be involved, and it is a great outreach project to the whole community. Instead of using the church building, tents and mock streets could be laid out in the parking lot or on the church lawn. An outdoor location makes using live animals more convenient. This event does call for lots of organization, such as:

▶ **Each person will need a script for dialogue to use when visitors pass their station.**

▶ **Guides should direct visitors through "Bethlehem" to the stable where Mary, Joseph, and the baby await.**

▶ **Set decorations, wardrobe, and "props" also will be needed:**
  painted cardboard and canvas backdrops, grain and bread for the baker, jewelry for the jeweler, cloth for the weaver, leather for the tanner, robes and other suitable clothing, assorted extension cords, lighting, and rolls of duct tape.

Before advertising the event, decide whether to collect a "love offering" or charge an entrance fee. Designate the money that is collected to go to a charity or Christmas outreach project.

One way to encourage participation from the entire congregation is to ask each Sunday school class or organization to be in charge of a particular "setting" on the streets in Bethlehem. Each year, add more streets and shops to your city of Bethlehem. Soon your youth may be able to say that they started a churchwide tradition.

Live Nativity

A live nativity scene is basically a smaller version of the Journey to Bethlehem. Usually held outdoors, the nativity is a live reenactment of the Christmas story as told in Luke and Matthew. You'll need:

- ☐ a stable,
- ☐ a manger,
- ☐ hay,
- ☐ live animals,
- ☐ lighting,
- ☐ actors/actresses,
- ☐ props,
- ☐ costumes,
- ☐ a star,
- ☐ a sound system to tell the story as the characters act out the drama.

An audio recording of the story, including appropriate background music at key points, will give the nativity a professional flair, and can be used year after year.

Advertise the performance as a free production for the community, and make sure adequate parking is available. If possible, present your live nativity within view of a well-traveled street, so passers-by can see what's happening and stop to watch.

Leave the scenery lighted and intact during nonproduction times, as a reminder to the community of the true meaning of Christmas.

New Years

Commitments

As your youth enter the new year, they will have their minds on the future. Tabloids boast of predictions for the new year; almanacs predict changes in weather patterns; and society affirms its new resolutions. The beginning of the year is an ideal time for teenagers to recommit their lives to Christ.

Offer a lock-in on New Year's Eve, complete with a commitment service. A lock-in provides a safe celebration alternative for your youth (away from wild parties and reckless drivers). Plan the lock-in to begin just before midnight, followed by a party to ring in the new year.

The commitment service is a place for youth to confess their shortcomings of the past year to God, to recognize God's forgiveness for those sins, to call on God's strength and help for the coming year, and to recommit to living a Christian life as a disciple of Christ. Consider adding a yearly goal for the group, such as bringing more youth into the community to Christ through invitations to church and youth meetings. If the minister is present for the service, close with communion, starting the year with the experience and understanding that Christ walks with us daily.

✹ ✹ ✹ ✹ ✹ Variation ✹ ✹ ✹ ✹ ✹

Hold a commitment service on the first Sunday of the new year, instead of on New Year's Eve.

Time Capsule

Plant a time capsule at the beginning of the new year, to be opened at a later date. Ask members of your group to write letters to themselves in the future, expressing their concerns, prayers, issues they are currently dealing with, the things that are important to them, favorite songs and movies, struggles with parents, and other current information. Seal the envelopes and place them in a waterproof container, along with recent newspaper and magazine articles. Consider including a videotape of your youth group and community in the "time capsule." Choose a little-used portion of the church grounds, dig a deep hole, and bury the capsule.

Decide how long the capsule should remain buried. Before reopening the capsule, contact everyone who contributed material and ask them to attend. Some groups open their capsule yearly, reviewing the past year and adding new information for the coming year. Or you could have a different capsule for each grade level. Open these capsules after each class's senior graduation. Use the occasion of opening the capsule for a discussion about the ways God has been involved in your students' issues and concerns in the past, and how this involvement will continue in the future.

Valentine's Day

The theme of Saint Valentine's Day is love, and it typically is a day when we recognize loved ones. It's only natural, then, that this day be one of celebrating God's love and our Christian love for one another. Try these ideas:

Sweetheart Dance

The youth at my church hold a traditional sweetheart dance each year. A dance committee composed of youth is organized each year to send out special invitations, plan the decorations and activities for the evening, organize the food, and line up the music—either a disk jockey or a live band. The admission price for couples or singles covers the cost of the event. The dance is a semiformal affair, and a professional photographer (a church member) is on hand to take pictures of the couples.

Valentine Cards

Make valentines for folks who are living in nursing homes or are patients in the hospital. Don't limit the recipients of the cards to just church members, but include extras that can be placed on the eating trays of all patients or residents.

Form a committee to gather glue, glitter, paper, doilies, markers, pens, pencils, yarn, and other art items that can be used for valentines. The various institutions should be contacted to determine where the cards should be delivered and how many cards will be needed.

Have everyone gather to make the valentines and recount the history of giving valentines. Divide the number of cards needed by the number of designers to determine the number of cards each person will need to make. Encourage creativity in the artwork and the written messages of God's love for each recipient.

When youth members deliver the cards, they will have an opportunity to meet and talk with some of the recipients. The next time Valentine's Day rolls around, they will remember an afternoon spent visiting with a stranger and spreading a little love.

Flower Bouquets

On every Valentine's Day, high schools around the country raise money for uniforms, the prom, or other important functions by selling flowers to "sweethearts." The giver pays a small fee to arrange for a carnation or rose to be delivered to his or her valentine—usually with an attached note from the giver.

Next time, order flowers to be delivered on Valentine's Day to each of your youth. Attach a message: "We at First Church want you to know we love you!" or "God loves you, and so does everyone at First Church!" For a scripture reference, use words from First Corinthians 13 (the love chapter) or Romans 8:35-39 (nothing can separate us from the love of God).

This activity can involve even the inactive youth in your group, because it pulls everyone into the fellowship. Nonmembers will learn about your congregation and about God's love from your youth as they walk around the school, carrying their flowers, and answering questions about who sent them.

Burning Sins

Burning sins on Ash Wednesday or during the Lenten season is a practice that has been common in the church for centuries. However, it may be unfamiliar to your youth group. Burning sins as a form of worship offers an experience of confession, as well as forgiveness. This activity allows Christians to offer their written sins to God, and then watch them literally be burned away through a flame—symbolic of the way the Holy Spirit burns away our sins.

Plan to have the worship service near a prepared bonfire, Sterno can, fireplace, grill, campfire, hole in the ground, or some other suitable place. Keep a fire extinguisher close at hand. Ask everyone to sit near the fire site.

Give a short talk about how we sin and fall short of God's plan. Distribute small slips of paper, asking each person to write about specific times when they have fallen short of God's plan for them. Explain the importance of actually writing the sin on the paper, that when we are up front with God about our shortcomings, we are better able to accept God's forgiveness for those sins. Allow time to pray regarding the sins that are acknowledged. Ask each individual to walk to the fire, place the paper in the flame, and watch the fire as his or her sins burn away. Afterward, remind everyone that just as the fire burned the paper, so the fire of God's Holy Spirit has burned away their sinfulness and cleansed them.

Variation

Instead of using plain paper, consider purchasing flash paper from a magic shop. At the slightest touch of the flame, this paper quickly disappears in a flash. It's safer and cleaner, since there is no lasting flame or ash.

Devotional Booklets

Often during Lent, Christians begin to study and read daily devotions. While this is a good discipline for any time of year, the season of Lent offers a set period of time for Christians to look inward at their unique walk with God and at the ways they have been asked to carry Christ's cross. Writing and printing devotional booklets for use by the entire church is an activity that can unite the congregational community during the Lenten season.

After the new year, ask a committee composed of youth to send out letters to 47 church members, including youth, adults, children, church staff, and volunteers. The number 47 symbolizes the 40 days of Lent, plus 7 Sundays, including Easter Sunday. Explain that the youth are compiling a devotion booklet. Ask the letter recipients to write a short, personal devotion based on a portion of scripture and ending with a prayer. The devotion can focus on a time when the writer felt especially close to God on a personal journey or during an experience, or on how the writer relates to God in his or her life. Be sure to inform the recipients of the date the devotions will be needed. The deadline should allow ample time for editing and printing the booklets. Announce to the congregation the date when the booklets will be available, and distribute them before Ash Wednesday.

This is an activity that draws generations together, and helps members understand one another and the Christian journey a little better.

Easter

A Sunrise Service

An Easter sunrise worship service is nothing new, but it can provide a new experience for your youth group. The level of youth participation in the service can vary from simple attendance to planning and leading the entire worship service.

If a sunrise service is not yet a part of your church's worship tradition, ask the pastor or worship committee if the youth could introduce and lead this service. Group members can meet with the pastor to plan a service that is creative, inspiring, and different from the usual Sunday morning worship service. Sunrise services often feature special music and a different way of presenting the morning message by utilizing drama, video, music, or the spoken word. Another easy variation is to invite someone other than the pastor to present the message, perhaps a congregation member or a teenager. Consider holding the service outdoors, so the sunrise can actually be seen during the service. Invite the entire church family, as well as the community.

If a sunrise service is already a part of your church's tradition, there are still ways that youth leadership and participation can be incorporated. Offer to be responsible for a particular part of the service, such as preparing the worship area, serving as ushers, providing music, or greeting worshipers. Your group may want to provide a breakfast following the service for early morning worshipers.

Even if the youth are unable to plan, lead, or participate in the service, they can attend worship together as a group.

Thanksgiving Cards

If we truly believe that the season of Thanksgiving should be spent giving thanks for God's blessings, why don't we spend more time thanking the people who have been blessings in our lives?

During the next Thanksgiving holiday, send thank-you letters or cards to parents, friends, mentors, relatives, ministers, teachers, or anyone else who has blessed the lives of the young people in your group. Gather as a group to make the cards or write the letters.

After all the cards and letters have been completed, have a brief worship time, thanking God for the blessing each person has provided.

Soup-Kitchen Servers

We can become more aware of our blessings by recognizing what life would be like without them. Ask your youth to serve a meal at a nearby homeless shelter or soup kitchen on Thanksgiving Day. It's a great way to allow God to use your youth group as blessings for others. In turn, you will be blessed with the knowledge that you are a tool of God, acting as the hands of Christ.

Daily Living

Teenagers receive a number of mixed messages about what constitutes adulthood. They are able to drive at 15 or 16, watch "R" rated movies at 17, vote and join the armed services at 18, and legally drink at 21. By intentionally incorporating celebrations that honor the achievements of your youth group members, you help teenagers recognize the various stepping-stones of responsibility toward adulthood.

I will bless the Lord at all times;
his praise shall continually be
in my mouth.

−Psalm 34:1

Confirmation

Confirmation is a long-standing custom celebrated in a number of church traditions. When a teenager is confirmed into the church, he or she accepts responsibility for his or her faith. Confirmation is a personal "confirming" of the vows made at baptism. It is an agreement to join a family of faith and be a part of the Body of Christ, the church.

Signing a Brick

Using symbols as part of the confirmation process helps to develop and strengthen the tradition of confirming one's baptismal vows. Just as each brick makes up a building, so each church member makes up the church. What if you were to have a brick or stone wall in your church, where youth would sign their names when they join the church? As years pass and children reach confirmation age, they will see the names of all the people who have made the same decision. When each brick has a name, start on a new wall, or use the same wall and add other names to the same bricks. Imagine, after years of this tradition, a child walking up to a brick and seeing his or her own parents' names! Some churches use a similar idea by painting a picture of the church building on the wall and asking students to draw themselves somewhere on the picture—looking out a window, hanging from a steeple, standing in a doorway, or waving from a car in the parking lot. The drawings can be simple stick figures, with a name written underneath. The artwork can adorn the wall until that class graduates, or it can be painted over for the next class.

Community Service Project

Sometimes confirmation classes choose a particular service project as a way of illustrating their contribution upon joining the faith family. As a class, decide:

1. what form of service to provide;
2. when the help will be offered; and
3. how to make the congregation aware of your project (that is, announce it during worship, during Sunday school classes, use a bulletin board, etc).

Some classes decide to adopt a particular project until they leave for college. These projects are a great way to experience "doing unto the least of these," as Christ commands.

Banquet

Churches confirm their youth in different ways and at different ages.

Some congregations confirm as a whole class, others do it individually, whenever the youth decides it is time to officially join the church. Classes may last only a few weeks, or several months. Then it's a time for celebration, perhaps even have a welcoming banquet into the church.

This is a unique way to involve the entire congregation in confirmation. Youth, adults, and children can gather to celebrate the newly professed Christians.

Plan your banquet for either the last Saturday before the class is confirmed, or if youth are confirmed at different times, decide on a specific date to recognize all the confirmands during the past year. Contact different people to be responsible for the different areas for the banquet one or two months in advance. Ask people from your congregation to plan:

► decorations (including centerpieces for the table);
► food (catered or covered dish);
► reservations (invite the families of the confirmands);
► gifts (symbolic and meaningful, but not expensive);
► program (consider having special music).

Make sure the senior pastor can attend, and invite the older youth to help serve or sit at each table.

Utilize as many different people as possible, including children, adults, staff, volunteers, clergy, parents, and teachers.

Mentors

Another way to involve adults in confirmation is through a mentoring program. This activity has the potential to build relationships that will last a lifetime.

One chief influential factor in a teenager becoming a Christian is a strong, healthy relationship with a Christian adult—in addition to parents. When one thousand youth at the 1994 Youth for Christ DC/LA Superconferences were asked why they "came to be Christian," they pointed to relationships with adult Christians and parents as their top motivators (*Group*, February 1995, pp. 18-22).

55 Group-Building Activities for Youth

Before you begin your confirmation training, ask each youth in the class for the name of an adult in the congregation whom they would like as a "mentor." The requirements of a mentor include:

▶ must be an adult member of the congregation who is not a parent of the youth;
▶ must attend the initial meeting with the confirmation student and parent, where class information is provided. This is also an opportunity for the mentor and student to get better acquainted;
▶ must pray for the student daily;
▶ must write a letter to the student to be delivered on confirmation Sunday, affirming the student and offering continued support;
▶ must sit with the student during worship at least two times before confirmation Sunday;
▶ must be mentor to only one student in the class.

Although not required, mentors often continue the support of their students after confirmation by attending youth activities and events, remembering birthdays, and sometimes even attending graduations.

Newsletters

Youth get excited over birthdays—especially when it's

their own. By publicly recognizing the birthdays of your youth group members, you are inviting the entire church community to participate in the celebration of those teenagers' lives.

Follow these steps to start a birthday tradition:

1. At each youth meeting, for about a month, ask the students to provide their names and birthdates on a sheet of paper.
2. List the names and birth dates in a monthly newsletter.
3. Send the newsletter to the youth or to the entire congregation at the beginning of each month. This provides everyone with ample time to send cards to the birthday boy or girl.

Sing at Meetings

At the beginning of each meeting, make a habit of asking whether anyone has celebrated a birthday since the last meeting. Then sing "Happy Birthday" to those people.

However, simply singing "Happy Birthday" isn't quite creative enough for most kids. So next time, try one of these ideas:

1. Ask the birthday boy or girl to stand on a chair in the center of the group.
2. Have the group sing while holding their tongues or not showing any teeth.
3. If your meeting is in a public place,

invite everyone to join in the singing.
4. Serenade the birthday person below his or her bedroom window after the meeting.

There are unlimited ways your group can add a touch of uniqueness to make birthdays more memorable.

Party a Month

During the last meeting of each month, throw a party for all the kids celebrating birthdays in that month. Send out special invitations and provide a cake as a part of the snack supper. Ask everyone to sign a birthday card for each person being recognized that month.

Videotape the parents of each birthday youth while they tell one or two stories about their son or daughter when they were young children. Play the recording at the party. By the end of the year you will have celebrated everyone's birthday and learned a little more about them, too.

Driving

Recognition Service

For teenagers, a driver's license symbolizes the point in their lives when they are considered responsible enough to operate a vehicle. One way to reinforce the responsibilty aspect of this achievement is to recognize new license holders in a special worship service held during a youth-meeting. Recognizing new drivers is a good way to connect this life achievement with the church community and the youth's own faith beliefs.

Plan the service for a meeting to be held *after* the license has been issued. (If you do it before, the youth may be terribly embarrassed if he or she doesn't pass the driving test.) Near the close of the meeting, gather around the license recipient in a meeting room, the parking lot, or even in the sanctuary, and repeat the following litany:

Leader: (Name of driver), you have entered a new phase of your life, different from any other. You are taking on a new responsibility, and with it comes the recognition by your parents, your community, and your state officials that you are responsible enough to be a driver. You are now expected to drive safely and thoughtfully, to think when you drive, to be willing to be responsible for all your actions behind the wheel. Do you accept this responsibility?

Driver: I do.

Leader: Do you realize that there are many younger than you who may be influenced by the attitude you have toward your driving, and do you still accept responsibility for those impressions?

Driver: I do.

Leader: Do you recognize that, as a driver, you have the keys to safety as well as danger, depending upon the way you drive your vehicle, and do you still accept the responsibility for trying to provide that safety for your community?

Driver: I do.

Leader: God has given you the ability and the gift to be able to function as a responsible driver behind the wheel. Do you accept God's guidance in this new role as a driver?

Driver: I do, and I pray that I will always follow such guidance.

Leader: I now turn to ask (name's) peers and family (if present), will you recognize this new driver as one who has chosen to drive responsibly and conscientiously in the years and miles ahead?

All: We will. And we pray that God will keep you safe on your road ahead. We respect your desire to be a safe driver and will do what we can to help you continue to drive responsibly.

After the litany, present the driver with a small gift. It might be a special key chain with a Christian symbol, a decal for the bumper or window, or any inexpensive gift that will remind the youth of the commitment to drive safely, and of the trust that he or she has earned.

Finally, close the meeting with a prayer, asking God to keep the driver safe on the roads that lie ahead, and remind-

ing the driver of the support and love that the church has for him or her.

Get-Well Wishes

Care Committee

Organize a committee of youth to be responsible for the ministry of delivering a gift to group members who are hospitalized or ill. This "membership care" committee can be trained in pastoral care and shown how they will be serving Christ by caring for the sick.

Visits

Instead of giving gifts to sick or hospitalized group members, try actually "being" the gift. Jesus said, "I was sick and you took care of me" (Matt. 25:36). When we serve one another, we serve Christ. Organize a group of youth who will visit ill youth members with you (or even without you). Depending upon the illness and the condition of the student being visited, suggest that the committee bring music, cards, food, or a game or two to pass the time. Be careful not to visit too long.

Not only is Christ being served when you visit those who are sick, but youth are helped by knowing that they are showing Christ to others.

Last Day of School

A Special Meal

Each year, the last day of school marks a new stage in the lives of your youth. Books are turned in, homework is finished, tests are over, summer plans await, and students claim the title of the next year's class.

Plan a special meal on this day of passage.

BREAKFAST

If you plan a breakfast, it will need to end before school starts on that last day. Offer a variety of food, and have the meal at a central location, such as the church or a home close to the school. Ask parents to help cook, drive, clean up, or just "hang out" with the youth during the breakfast. This is also a good time to publicize upcoming summer programs and activities.

LUNCH

Sponsoring a lunch may be a little more difficult, since many kids may not be allowed to leave their school campus. If this is the case, you will need to secure special permission from school officials. Find out when the youth need to be back at school, and then advertise the lunch in as many ways as possible (consider the school newspaper, if you want to include nonchurch youth). Take reservations and hold the lunch at the church or a nearby restaurant. Make sure the youth get back to class on time.

DINNER

A fancy dinner can last longer than the other two meals, since the school day will already be finished. Have this meal at the church or in a home. Some churches offer a different dinner for each grade level in separate locations, and a special meal for graduates. (See also "Graduation Banquet" below.) Set the registration deadline for a month before the dinner, in order to know how much food to prepare (or order), and the amount of space you will need. Check with students before inviting parents and other family members, since the youth may want to have their own night out with their friends to mark this special occasion.

Graduation

Graduation Banquet

One way to link the achievement milestone of graduation to the church is to hold a graduation banquet each year.

The banquet can be held at the church, in someone's home, or in a reserved section of a restaurant. Invite the graduating seniors, various church staff, and adult volunteers who have worked with the graduates. Parents and other family members of the graduates also can be invited. The banquet program might feature a guest speaker, parents recounting stories about their kids, or slides from past youth events.

✿ ✿ ✿ ✿ ✿ Variation ✿ ✿ ✿ ✿ ✿

1. Instead of a program, consider offering a simple social evening that allows lots of time for the graduates to talk about future plans.

2. Make the banquet a classy affair. Use fine linen tablecloths, fancy decorations, elegant dishes, and outstanding food. Ask the new graduates to dress in their most stylish outfits for the event. Enlarge a variety of photographs featuring the graduates, and scatter them throughout the room.

Legacy Wall

This idea is similar to the brick signing in the confirmation section. One Sunday during the month when the majority of high school graduations will occur, invite all the graduating students to attend Sunday school. Prepare a lesson that will be especially meaningful to them. Take a photo of the graduates, and ask each one to sign a brick in a designated wall. The wall symbolizes that they are a part of the structure of the church—a member of the Body of Christ.

A Gift to the Church

Senior classes typically present their school with a class gift, to remind future students, the school staff, and alumni of the impact that class had on the school. Flagpoles, benches, water fountains, clocks, scoreboards, and goal posts are just a few of the kinds of gifts that have been donated to schools as a result of this tradition.

The seniors in your youth group can initiate this practice in your congregation. The class members should start raising money or making contributions toward the gift in February or March. In a letter to all the seniors, describe the project and how it provides an opportunity to help their church continue to influence the lives of youth in the future. Suggest possible ideas that would make appropriate gifts to be presented to the church on the Sunday before or after the last day of school. Gift suggestions might include:

▶ a nicely framed painting
▶ audio/video equipment
▶ furniture
▶ a pew in the sanctuary or chapel
▶ a picture window
▶ playground equipment

▶ a pulpit Bible
▶ books for the church library
▶ a music stand for the choir loft
▶ a scholarship fund for youth who cannot afford youth retreats
▶ a special chalice and plate for serving communion on youth trips
▶ Bibles or hymnals for the sanctuary

Ask the church to purchase a plaque for the donated item which lists the year donated and the name of the graduating class. Unlike the school, the church is a place that the graduates will be returning to again and again. They will be remembered, and their contributions—physical, spiritual, and congregational—will continue to enrich the fellowship of believers.

Community Service Project

Imagine the impact that would occur if the graduating seniors in your congregation and community adopt a practice of being in mission and service for others. As disciples of Christ, we are called to serve others. Begin encouraging your seniors to look outward into the community to find a community service project to adopt before they graduate (or during the summer following graduation).

Organize a group of three to five seniors to contact social service agencies in your area to help them determine some of the needs in your community, such as:

▶ individual families or housing developments that need child care;
▶ single family homes that need physical repair;
▶ students who need tutors;
▶ a community park near a low-income residential district that needs fixing up.

These are just a few possible avenues for service in every community. Asking seniors to give back to their community may give them a taste of service that they never before have experienced. It certainly will provide an opportunity to experience Christ in new ways.

Influencing Traditions

Teenagers establish their own set of guidelines, which usually have little to do with the church. Often these include, but are not limited to:

▶ where to hang out;
▶ who to hang out with;
▶ going to the prom;
▶ where to sit at football games;
▶ what to do at school events;
▶ where to go for summer and spring break vacations

Here are some ideas that can help you involve your youth ministry in the daily events and happenings in your teenagers' lives:

Photo Shoot

Kids often like to dress up and spend a special evening out with a date. Prom night,

homecoming, or a school dinner and dance are just a few of the special events or functions that occur during the school year.

The next time one of these events occurs, organize a photo shoot. Ask a few of the parents to host a photo shoot in one or more homes. Limit the number of couples to ten per house. Provide light snacks that can be enjoyed after the picture-taking. Have the couples arrive ready to take pictures in front of a creative backdrop (i.e., spring flowers in the garden, a long staircase in the entryway, a deck out back, or a sunny front lawn). Invite the parents of all the party-going couples to bring their cameras and attend.

Friday Nights

For teenagers, Friday night is often the time for getting together with a group of friends, trying to cram in as much socializing as possible before curfew.

In order to get your church involved with teenagers, you will need to:

1. Find out where they spend their Friday nights. Do they frequent school sporting events, particular malls, cinemas, restaurants, or fast food places?
2. Think of creative ways to introduce your church to the kids who frequent those locations:

▶ During football or basketball season, run an ad in the school program, listing the location and time of your youth group meetings. Ask one or two of the youth who attend the school if you can include their pictures in the ad.
▶ Print a huge banner with a message

that encourages the team, lets everyone know that God loves them, and mentions the name of the church. Ask school officials about hanging the banner on the fence around the football field or in the school gymnasium during basketball season.

▶ Organize teams of adult leaders to visit a popular mall every Friday night. The team members can spend a few minutes talking to the kids while they are "hanging out."

▶ Movie theaters usually run ads before the beginning of each movie. Ask the management to show a public service announcement about your weekly youth meetings during that time.

▶ Fast-food restaurants often give coupons to churches to be used at their discretion. Print the name of the church on the coupons, and use them as prizes for games and events during youth meetings.

▶ Find out which radio stations your kids listen to, and run public service announcements or advertisements on Friday nights during the peak listening hours.

Remember that the intent of these suggestions is to influence the lives of young people through ministry, so . . .

. . . Rather than placing a typical "advertisement" in the football program, print a portion of scripture with an invitation to the fellowship your church offers.

. . . Use the radio or movie theater public-service announcements to remind kids that their bodies are temples of God and should not be abused by alcohol or drugs.

CHAPTER 6

Connecting
the Old and the New

The church is full of ancient traditions that have been passed down from generation to generation since the time of the apostles. Communion, baptism, foot washing, and professing one's faith are just a few of the religious practices that are meaningful to millions of Christians throughout the world. Finding ways to give meaning to these traditional practices for the youth in your church will provide a wellspring for them to draw upon as they explore and strengthen their individual faith.

Because there is one bread,
we who are many are one body,
for we all partake of the one bread.

–1 Corinthians 10:17

Communion

All Christians recognize the Lord's Supper as a sacrament. John Wesley, the founder of Methodism, believed that a Christian should partake of communion as often as possible. In some congregations, communion is offered every day; in others, every week; a significant number offer it monthly or quarterly. Unfortunately, many congregants do not realize the significance of communion.

Teenagers are sometimes disinterested in communion because they view it as a ritual, with lots of motions, fancy words, kneeling, and "proper" ways to do things, but with little real meaning.

To counter these views creatively, offer the sacrament during youth worship by:

▶ using youth oriented music;

▶ utilizing different types of coverings (i.e., tablecloth, fabric remnant), breads (i.e., a loaf, wafers), and cups (i.e., individual cups, a chalice) on the communion table;

▶ calling the youth by name as they take the sacrament;

▶ asking the youth to prepare or help serve the elements. Perhaps they could bake the bread or make the juice used in the ceremony.

While away on a retreat, find interesting places to enjoy the Lord's Supper—an upper room in an old recreation hall, a dark cellar lit with candles, a mountaintop at sunrise, a foggy beach at dawn, or a boat on a lake. Explain that Christ gave us the gift of communion with him, in a form that enables us to celebrate it anywhere, just as we can experience Christ anywhere. Communion symbolizes that we are all one Body of Christ, and as we partake of the sacrament, we are connecting to the rest of the congregation and the worldwide Christian family.

Baptism

Baptism is another ancient tradition that is a holy sacrament. It is a symbol of God's grace, which abides with everyone.

Throughout the Bible, water is used to symbolize cleansing oneself, quenching thirst, and destroying a sinful world. Water was also used:

▶ at Jesus' baptism;
▶ to destroy a sinful world in the time of Noah;
▶ to wash Pilot's hands of the guilt of Jesus' death; and
▶ by Jesus to symbolize a cup that is never empty, when

describing himself to the Samaritan woman at the well.

Discuss these and other symbols of water in the Bible.

Plan a traditional "baptismal remembering" time at your next retreat. Ask each person to touch or splash in water, remembering that God washes away their sins, just as the water washes us clean. At the time the youth touch the water, say, "Remember your baptism" (if they have already been baptized), helping them link water with God's grace, which is symbolized by baptism.

Talk about your own baptism. Give specific details, such as:

> ▶ who was there
> ▶ the pastor's name
> ▶ what it felt like (if you remember)
> ▶ why you were baptized.

Ask the youth to tell about their baptism experiences. If they were baptized as infants, encourage them to ask their parents about the event. Be sensitive to students who have not yet chosen to be baptized. Baptism is very sacred and should be entered into when an individual and the Holy Spirit are ready.

Sometimes a youth will want to be baptized while you are on a retreat. This is often quite moving, and makes worship a very memorable experience. However, before conducting a baptism, consider the young person's family and the rest of the church family who may wish to be a part of the ceremony. One option is to invite everyone who attended the retreat to your church on the next Sunday, to witness and participate in the baptism while the entire congregation is gathered.

Foot Washing

For many people, foot washing is too uncomfortable or embarrassing to engage in regularly. After all, who wants to go through the hassle and humility of taking off their shoes and socks or hose to let a stranger touch their feet? Nevertheless, Jesus introduced foot washing to the church and instructed his disciples to perform it for each other.

In washing someone's feet, we recognize our role as servants of the world. Jesus, our Savior, humbled himself to wash the feet of his disciples, setting an example for all Christians—to serve each other. In so serving, we serve Christ. In so receiving, we receive from the hands of Christ—from the Body of Christ.

Read John 13:1-20, and if your group is resistant to foot washing, identify other ways they can serve each other:

> ▶ massage each other's shoulders;
> ▶ wash each other's hands;
> ▶ dust each other's shoes; or
> ▶ serve food to each other.

Practice this activity once a month, at every retreat, or on mission trips where service is a key element of the experience. As the scripture becomes more familiar and teenagers become more experienced with serving, they will begin to identify other ways of serving people in their congregation and community.

Don't be afraid to move ahead with the practice of foot washing, even if your kids feel uncomfortable. Remind them that the disciples also felt uncomfortable. They would have been happy to wash Jesus' feet, but felt embarrassed and unworthy to have him wash theirs. Use the discomfort of your youth as a springboard into making this scripture come alive for them, emphasizing that sometimes we are embarrassed when we must have our sins washed clean by Christ.

Corporate Worship

While it is important that youth in the church experience their own times of worship on retreats and at regular youth meetings, it is also important for them to participate in corporate worship. Christians need the fellowship of intergenerational worship. When children, parents, young and older adults, and teenagers meet to celebrate the Risen Christ, they encounter a tradition and an experience that cannot be found in age-segregated worship. The old need the young to remind them that the kingdom of heaven belongs to the children; the young need the old to be told the age-old stories and learn from the experience of their elders; the children need the youth, who can remember what it was like to be that small; the youth need the children, who view them as leaders and look at them differently than do adults.

Find ways to include members of the youth group into the corporate worship experience:

▶ Sit together in a special place in the sanctuary.
▶ Invite the youth choir to sing the anthem.
▶ Use teenagers as soloists or liturgists.
▶ Use songs, poems, sayings, or benedictions familiar to youth.

Following are other ways to include youth in corporate worship:

Ushers

Although many congregations follow a practice of inviting young people to serve as ushers on a particular Sunday during the month or year, consider using both youth and adults as ushers throughout the year. This encourages the two age groups to work together. Isn't that what we are to do in the Body of Christ?

Prayer

An individual or a particular class in the youth group could be asked to write a prayer or litany for the Sunday service. This activity could culminate a discussion or program on a particular topic featured at a previous youth meeting.

Ask the youth to pray for the worship leaders. Since prayer increases one's interest in those being prayed for, teenagers will begin to recognize how God is using their prayers for the whole congregation.

Fasting

Fasting is not practiced as much as it once was. The majority of teenagers fast only in an effort to fit into a swimsuit for next week's trip to the beach, to lose weight in order to make the team, or as a method of sleeping an extra thirty minutes before going to school each morning.

Try fasting as a spiritual discipline. Your group members may find themselves leading the rest of your congregation into trying this discipline.

In *Celebration of Discipline,* Richard Foster says that fasting reveals the things that control us. He explains that when we abstain from something we have come to depend upon, we recognize the feelings or priorities that are in control. Pride, anger, jealousy—these things come to the surface when we no longer can rely on other things to hide them. But this awareness of what controls us is good for us, because we know that healing is available through Christ.

Young people have many things in their lives that can keep them from realizing what controls them—television, cars, friends, ath-

letic teams, food, clothes. These things cloud their vision and keep them from recognizing the underlying anger, rage, lust, pride, or jealousy. When the veil is removed, teenagers are more likely to recognize that food, clothing, friends, or television are not enough—that God is the true sustainer.

The purpose of fasting is not for a better understanding of self, a better prayer life, or a greater spirituality. Fasting is, first and foremost, a form of worship, to glorify God. Otherwise, says Foster, we end up loving the blessing more than the blesser, who is God.

It is best to introduce a fast slowly. Discuss the true meaning and purpose of fasting, and offer guidelines for participating in a fast. Two excellent resources are available to help you get started—*Celebration of Discipline* (Foster's book), and *Fasting: A Neglected Discipline,* by David Smith.

Introduce the fast during the season of Lent, since traditionally, Christians are asked to go without something for forty days during that time. Encourage students to go without soft drinks, junk foods, television, snacks, or desserts. The chosen item should be something that is eaten, drunk, or practiced regularly. Be sure to explain the reason that Sundays are not fasting days, but times to celebrate Christ's resurrection.

Make sure your youth understand that they should not go on a total food fast. They may wish to give up a lunch or a certain type of food (such as red meat or sweets), but remind them to eat plenty of other nutrients in place of what they give up.

During the fast, offer a weekly Bible study or a prayer meeting at the church. After the fast, discuss the experience and how God was glorified.

Prayer

It's not unusual that the disciples asked Jesus how to pray (Luke 11). Even today, many people don't believe they really know how they should pray to God. Teenagers sometimes feel awkward when praying because it is fairly new to them. Like the disciples, they often need direction in learning how to talk to God.

Introducing prayer in your group may be slow at first, or even difficult. Just as beginning a conversation with a new student can be awkward, so can starting a practice of talking with God. Explain this to your youth. Help them realize that even in their own prayer times, they may not be sure of what to say to God, but time will change that.

1. *Use every opportunity to incorporate prayer into your youth meetings:*

   ▶ Begin each gathering with a short prayer.
   ▶ Pray before every meal.
   ▶ Pray before leaving for a youth retreat.
   ▶ Close each youth meeting with a prayer.

At first, offer the prayers yourself. Next, invite one or two youth to offer a prayer during one of your regular prayer times. The opening prayer of a meeting is a good time to simply ask, "Would anyone like to give the prayer tonight?" After the prayer, thank the prayer giver. Don't worry if the prayer isn't flowery or fancy or even smooth or organized. The fact that someone was willing to talk to God out loud in front of the rest of the group, and on behalf of the whole group, is a great start. Youth need to know

that they can talk to God at any time and in any way.

During the closing prayer at youth meetings, try leading the prayer, then offering time for the youth to express their concerns out loud. They may wish to state only a person's name or a situation. Afterward, continue by asking God to hear the prayers stated "aloud as well as silently."

Consider using the altar rail in your closing worship time. Explain that the altar is available for anyone who wishes to come and pray. To help youth become more accustomed to coming to the altar, ask them to come as a group for communion, to drop a note in a basket, or for some other ritual. Eventually, you can simply offer the time at the altar while a song is softly played or sung. As the altar is made available each week, you may find more and more youth coming to spend some personal time with God. This will lead to your youth willingly and easily kneeling at the altar during the regular worship hour.

2. *Offer a weekly study on prayer only for those who are interested,* to help them begin to build a personal prayer life. This is not like the regular weekly meeting. Focus the topics on the various types of prayer:

   ▶ personal prayer,
   ▶ interceding prayers,
   ▶ sung prayers,
   ▶ group prayers, and
   ▶ prayers in the Bible.

In addition, discuss why the youth pray, when they pray, what they pray for, and what happens (or doesn't happen) when they pray. Introduce the practice of keeping a prayer journal, in which they will spend two to five months writing their prayer requests in a book. Later, when they look back through their journal, they can see what happened to those prayers after they were lifted to God.

3. *Start a "Secret Prayer Partner" program.* This is similar to the confirmation mentoring program, except that here the youth do *not* choose their partners.

Begin the program by sending a letter to each youth, explaining the program and asking for their participation. Participants should register by using a form similar to the one below.

Name: _____

School: _____

Address: _____

_____

Phone Number: _____

Birthday: _____

Family members living in the home: _____

_____

Names of favorite friends: _____

_____

_____

Hobbies and interests: _____

_____

How free time is spent: _____

_____

_____

Prayer requests or concerns: _____

_____

_____

_____

Next, contact several adults and ask them to volunteer. Plan on having the same number of adults as the youth who have registered. At an organizational meeting, assign the secret youth partners and explain to the adults their responsibilities:

► pray for your youth partner daily;

► write one or more short notes to your partner each week (the program can last as long as you'd like, but begin with about six weeks);

► keep your identity a mystery;

► be supportive of your youth partner by keeping track of special days, events, retreats, and significant occurrences in his or her life;

► give a small, inexpensive gift every week or so, to help lift the spirits of your youth partner *(optional)*.

This program affirms not only the youth, but also the adults, who witness the power that prayer can make in a young person's life. It also helps the entire congregation to more fully understand the significance of prayer, while creating a unique, meaningful solidarity between youth and adults.

As prayer becomes a habit in the lives of your young people, they will begin to immediately look to God whenever they feel in need. And they will know that God is always there.

Scripture

While scripture may be heard weekly in your youth meetings, it may not be respected or revered as the holy Word that it is. Imagine a youth group that respects the reading and hearing of God's Word. When scripture is read and heard with reverence, it is more likely to be followed with the same reverence and respect. Visitors who see friends showing respect for God's Word at youth meetings are more likely to wonder what these words say and what they mean to their friends.

However, these should not be the only reasons for developing a reverence for scripture. Reverence should be instilled simply because scripture is the Word of God. It is holy, and that holiness should not be used as a tool to "get" people to act a certain way. We act in certain ways, rather, because the Word is given to us by God. A response of respect is just that—a response to a message that is written for us and is eternally meaningful. As your youth see that reverence is a response to the scripture, and not a gimmick to make them quiet or show piety, then the Holy Spirit can be more fully involved in your study and worship, and your youth will be more likely to respond out of faith. Here are several ideas to try:

Offer a scripture reading each week during a brief worship service. Gather in the sanctuary, a chapel, outdoors, or in a particular classroom. Before reading the scripture, light a candle and sing one verse of a hymn or recite a prayer. This announces to the worshipers that it is time for the scripture reading. Ask the person reading the scripture to stand. This action signifies the importance of God's Word to the worshipers. Consider adding a congregational response, such as:

Leader: This is the Word of God for the people of God.
All: Thanks be to God. Amen.

The scriptures were written to be read aloud

and heard by a group of people. During a weekly youth meeting, read a portion of the scripture. Then ask someone else to read it again. Explain that you want everyone to hear the scripture in different tones of voice. Since every person reads in a different way, perhaps the listener will hear the message in a different way as well. Finally, read the passage in unison.

As opportunities arise, use different ways of reading and listening to the Word, such as:

▶ Act out a parable as it is read.
▶ Sign the scripture reading while it is being read aloud.
▶ Read every other verse responsively, alternating between groups (i.e., one side of the room with the other, boys and girls, leader and congregation).

▶ Sing a psalm in a chant style. Sing the same note for an entire line. Then, on the next to last word in the line, move up or down one note.

As youth see that particular attention is given to the reading and hearing of the scripture, they too will begin to pay special attention to these words. Soon they will begin asking questions about what makes scripture so special.

Offer a Bible study. As teenagers begin to recognize the sanctity and sacredness of scripture, they will need guidance on how to interpret it. Consider inviting different church members of various ages to the study sessions to share their insights and experiences.

CHAPTER 7

Adapting Negative Customs

A few of the ongoing practices that youth have adopted may be unsafe, unhealthy, harmful to others, disrupting to the youth ministry program, or against Christian beliefs. Rather than ignoring these behaviors or labeling a teenager a "lost cause," try reshaping the custom to make it more beneficial.

The changing of negative behaviors and patterns is actually rooted in Christian history. Some Christian holidays resulted from missionary encounters with pagan ceremonies, later remolded into Christian celebrations. The druids' celebration for the dead, which occurred on the last day of October, was reformed to create All Saints' Day, when faithful servants of God are celebrated.

Several examples of negative youth traditions are outlined, along with creative suggestions for turning them into positive, affirming practices.

Come, O Children, listen to me;
   I will teach you the fear of the LORD.
Which of you desires life,
   and covets many days to enjoy good?
Keep your tongue from evil,
   and your lips from speaking deceit.
Depart from evil, and do good;
   seek peace, and pursue it.

–Psalm 34:11-14

The Back Pew

Perhaps your group has adopted this tradition of sitting together on the back pew, but you have found that they become loud and unruly during worship. You may also have noticed a few of them sneaking out of the sanctuary during the sermon—an easy thing to do, since they are sitting behind their parents. Rather than trying to kill a vital custom, think of alternative ways to affirm their decision to sit together. You can even affirm their decision to sit in the same place every Sunday by asking them to move to the front pew. There, they will be noticed by the entire congregation as having claimed a place in the fellowship of Christ. This solution may not result in a permanent change, but it will help curtail inappropriate habits, while still supporting your group's desire for togetherness.

Keg Parties

Keg parties (i.e., beer bashes, drinking parties, etc.) typically occur throughout the school year, and contribute to a significant number of teenage fatalities. Try these suggestions to counter this harmful practice:

1. Stay informed about what's happening with the youth in your congregation. Get on the school mailing list to receive copies of the school newsletter. Communicate regularly with a school counselor, teacher, or administrator to learn about the upcoming "social events" your kids are talking about.

2. Volunteer to be a chaperon, or ask other adults from your congregation to volunteer. If your youth attend an event and see you or another church member there, they will be reminded of

their responsibility as Christians. In addition, these events can provide good discussion topics for your youth meetings.

3. The *real* reason kids like to party is to get together with their friends and have a good time. So plan a party, and invite all the teenagers in the community. Show them that they can have a good time without alcohol. Provide music, food, and a place to "hang out" for a few hours after a football game, a dance, or on any ol' Friday night.

4. Some communities offer "After Prom" or "After Graduation" parties, where an amusement park or club is rented, complete with a band or disk jockey. Tons of great door prizes (stereos, CD's, dinners for two) donated by local merchants are awarded. The parties are publicized for several weeks in advance to get the word out to "everyone." These parties are great places for a youth minister or volunteer adult to serve as a chaperon.

The kids are told that if they leave the party early, their parents will be called. Teenagers who have been drinking alcohol are not admitted. These types of parties are fun, safe alternatives to the traditional drink-fests.

5. Offer an "open gym" night every Friday. Use the gym for late night basketball or volleyball games. Ask several adults from your church to volunteer as chaperons. Establish a set of rules and offer snacks throughout the night.

Sneaking Out

This is a favorite challenge on youth retreats, conferences, or trips. When the lights are out and the adults are asleep, it's risky and exciting to try to sneak away—even if there's really no place to go.

There are ways to safely and creatively defeat the challenge of sneaking out in your retreat. For example:

▶ Have a meeting prior to the retreat with the adults in your group, telling them they are allowed to "instigate" a time to sneak out one night after curfew. The adult and youth who sneak out could pull some practical joke (not damaging to property or embarrassing to any individual) that your group will talk about for months or years.

▶ Set up a few surprises for the group of youth who are sneaking out. Have one or two adults instigate the night out, while the other adults set up a few traps or surprises for the night owls. One youth minister placed adults in trees with buckets of water balloons. As the youth made their way through the woods, they were bombarded with balloons, yet they had had no idea that the adults were in the trees overhead, watching and listening. Another group of adults took a small group of boys out on a "snipe hunt" after curfew. They also planted an adult on top of a hill, waving a rifle and yelling "get off my land." The boys never got over a fence so quickly before, and continued to laugh and talk about that night for years.

Remember to always discourage teenagers from sneaking out on their own. In fact, discipline for those who do should be clear and swift, and occur immediately after the incident is discovered. Prior to the retreat, you should outline steps that may be taken: *calling a youth's parent in the middle of the night; sending a repeat offender home; asking parents to take their child home separately from the rest of the group on the last day; banning a youth from the next retreat; moving a youth to a special room with two adults for the rest of the weekend*—all these are ways you can respond to those who sneak out.

Sometimes parents also may be struggling with kids who are sneaking out of the house at night. Sponsor a parent/youth forum at a youth meeting on "sneaking out." Discuss the reasons for this practice and the potential problems that might arise.

Swirlys

Who would have thought that the practice of turning a youth upside down, sticking his or her head in a toilet, and flushing would become an honored routine? You may find, though, that after some of your youth experience a "swirly" (as they are affectionately called), they may proudly brandish their new, pointed hairstyle to every friend in camp, before hitting the showers.

This activity, which usually occurs on retreats or trips, can be either damaging or uplifting to the recipient. Meet with the youth who are leaders in your group before the retreat and ask them to intervene in any potentially hurtful situations. For example, a swirly may be great fun for someone who likes practical jokes, but if the student is quiet and shy, this may be interpreted as a cruel hoax.

Fire Drills

A "fire drill" occurs when a van, car, or bus load of teenagers stop at a traffic light, and suddenly the doors fly open. Everyone in the vehicle gets out and runs around the vehicle, waving their arms, screaming and laughing. When the light changes, everyone scurries back into the

car as the other traffic begins to move, and they drive off—safely, we hope.

There are some ways to salvage this activity. The next time someone in your vehicle yells "fire" while on a road trip:

1. Pull immediately into the nearest fast-food place, drive up to the window, and have everyone get out and run around the vehicle, saying, "Have a nice day" or "Just wanted to stop by and say 'hi'" as they run past the window.

2. Stop at a gas station and have everyone run around a pump island (or the entire building). You might even start a trend of having a fire drill every time your group passes the same fast-food place, convenience store, or corner parking lot. Pick a place close to the church, so that it happens fairly often. For good public relations, visit the manager of the establishment to explain what's going on.

CHAPTER 8

Discovering
Your Group's Traditions

To determine what activities and events occur regularly in your youth group, make a list. Use the charts titled *Youth Group* and *Church* in the Appendix to list the various ongoing activities that take place throughout the year.

[God] removes every branch in me
that bears no fruit.
Every branch that bears fruit he prunes
to make it bear more fruit.

–John 15:2

For the chart titled *Youth Group,* think about the activities that occur regularly in your youth group (i.e., Bible study, summer trip/outing, Thankgiving baskets, etc.). List these under the first column (see sample on page 85). You may be surprised at the length of this list. After a week, review the list and add any events or activities you might have missed earlier.

Now in the second column, note the benefits of each tradition. Answer these questions for each item listed:

> ▶ What person, people, or group is affected by this tradition?
> ▶ What is the effect?
> ▶ Is the effect positive or negative?
> ▶ What do the youth learn from this activity?
> ▶ Do newcomers feel welcome, or like outsiders?

These are important questions as you determine the benefits. Every tradition has a benefit. Perhaps the kids find a common interest or discover new friends.

Total the number of benefits you listed for all the activities, and write that number at the bottom of the column. Add a plus sign (+) next to that number.

Under the next column, write the number of times the activity occurs throughout the year (i.e., weekly, daily, annually, etc.).

In column four, list any negative results of the activity (i.e., youth disrupt the worship service, managers of businesses become angry, visitors feel left out, dangerous, etc.). Ask yourself the same questions you asked under column two. Total the number of negatives at the bottom of the column, with a minus (−) sign.

We hope the positives outweigh the negatives. Realize, though, that a regular practice may have one powerful benefit and three minor drawbacks. This is why the next column is so important.

In the final column, list strategies to curtail the negatives listed in column four. Note the phone numbers of people who may need to be called, addresses if letters need to be mailed, or specific directions for the other adult leaders. Make this a working list, which can be modified easily in the months ahead.

Now move to the chart titled *Church.* Under the first column, list the customs and practices that are a part of the life of your church, such as worship, communion, baptism, a special song sung at a certain event or time during worship, an activity performed at Christmas, or a statement or phrase that is made to new members (see sample on page 86). In the second column, list the ways your youth are involved in those traditions. Leave a blank place next to the ones in which youth do not participate. Your goal is to find ways to fill those blank spaces. By helping teenagers connect with a strong, effective church custom, you help them form a closer tie to the church body. The more involved they become in the larger church community, the less likely they are to feel like a separate entity of the Body of Christ.

Ask the other members of the youth staff for their comments and feedback, which may uncover other benefits or negatives that are not listed on the two charts. Each year, as the youth leadership team assesses the youth program and plans for the coming year, review these charts, adapting them as new customs or practices develop.

As you review the charts, think about new ideas or activities that you might like to introduce to your youth and congregation. Read through the pages of this book again and again. As the students in your group change, so will the group's habits and routines. One new experience will open the door to others, each offering the potential for stronger unity and community in your youth ministry.

As you encounter new activities and experiences in your youth group, remember that these are the ways traditions are started. It may not be easy to let go of long-standing practices for something new, but your youth may be honing and breaking in a new tradition, unique and significant to your group alone. Allow this to happen. Whether unconsciously or consciously, your youth may be instigating something they feel has been missing. If this new activity develops into an ongoing practice, it will connect them to one another, to the church (present, past, and future), and—most especially—to God.

Youth Activities	Benefits	Frequency	Negatives	Strategies for Change
Thanksgiving Baskets	Helps Families for Food	Annually		
Spring and Fall Retreats	Teaches youth service	Twice a year	Youth sneak out	

Total Benefits:

Total Negatives:

Congregational Activities	Youth Participation
Worship	ushers, liturgist, offertory stewards
Baptism	
Christmas Toy Drive	collect toys and books

Appendix

Youth Activities	Benefits	Frequency	Negatives	Strategies for Change

Total Benefits:

Total Negatives:

From *55 Group-Building Activities for Youth* by Sam Halverson. Copyright © 1996 by Abingdon Press. Permission to photocopy granted for local church use only.

Congregational Activities	Youth Participation

From *55 Group-Building Activities for Youth* by Sam Halverson. Copyright © 1996 by Abingdon Press. Permission to photocopy granted for local church use only.

Index